DEADLY DISEASES AND EPIDEMICS

POLIO

Second Edition

DEADLY DISEASES AND EPIDEMICS

DEADLY DISEASES AND EPIDEMICS

POLIO

Second Edition

Alan Hecht, D.C.

CONSULTING EDITOR
Hilary Babcock, M.D., M.P.H.,
Infectious Diseases Division,
Washington University School of Medicine,
Medical Director of Occupational Health (Infectious Diseases),
Barnes-Jewish Hospital and St. Louis Children's Hospital

FOREWORD BY
David Heymann
World Health Organization

616.835
H447

CHELSEA HOUSE
P U B L I S H E R S
An imprint of Infobase Publishing

Deadly Diseases and Epidemics: Polio, Second Edition

Copyright © 2009 by Infobase Publishing

Chelsea House
An imprint of Infobase Publishing
132 West 31st Street
New York, NY 10001

Library of Congress Cataloging-in-Publication Data
Hecht, Alan.
  Polio / Alan Hecht ; foreword by David Heymann. -- 2nd ed.
    p. cm. -- (Deadly diseases and epidemics)
  Includes bibliographical references and index.
  ISBN-13: 978-1-60413-238-0 (alk. paper)
  ISBN-10: 1-60413-238-8 (alk. paper)
  1. Poliomyelitis--Juvenile literature. 2. Poliomyelitis--History--Juvenile litera-
ture. I. Title. II. Series.

  RC180.1.H43 2008
  616.8'35--dc22
                          2008035806

Series design by Terry Mallon
Cover design by Keith Trego

Printed in the United States of America

Bang EJB 10 9 8 7 6 5 4 3 2 1

This book is printed on acid-free paper.

Table of Contents

Foreword

Communicable diseases kill and cause long-term disability. The microbial agents that cause them are dynamic, changeable, and resilient: They are responsible for more than 14 million deaths each year, mainly in developing countries.

Approximately 46 percent of all deaths in the developing world are due to communicable diseases, and almost 90 percent of these deaths are from AIDS, tuberculosis, malaria, and acute diarrheal and respiratory infections of children. In addition to causing great human suffering, these high-mortality communicable diseases have become major obstacles to economic development. They are a challenge to control either because of the lack of effective vaccines, or because the drugs that are used to treat them are becoming less effective because of antimicrobial drug resistance.

Millions of people, especially those who are poor and living in developing countries, are also at risk from disabling communicable diseases such as polio, leprosy, lymphatic filariasis, and onchocerciasis. In addition to human suffering and permanent disability, these communicable diseases create an economic burden—both on the work force that handicapped persons are unable to join, and on their families and society, upon which they must often depend for economic support.

Finally, the entire world is at risk of the unexpected communicable diseases, those that are called emerging or re-emerging infections. Infection is often unpredictable because risk factors for transmission are not understood, or because it often results from organisms that cross the species barrier from animals to humans. The cause is often viral, such as Ebola and Marburg hemorrhagic fevers and severe acute respiratory syndrome (SARS). In addition to causing human suffering and death, these infections place health workers at great risk and are costly to economies. Infections such as Bovine Spongiform Encephalopathy (BSE) and the associated new human variant of Creutzfeldt-Jakob Disease (vCJD) in Europe, and avian influenza A (H5N1) in Asia, are reminders of the seriousness of emerging and re-emerging infections. In addition, many of these infections have the potential to cause pandemics, which are a constant threat our economies and public health security.

Science has given us vaccines and anti-infective drugs that have helped keep infectious diseases under control. Nothing demonstrates the effectiveness of vaccines better than the successful eradication of smallpox, the decrease in polio as the eradication program continues, and the decrease in measles when routine immunization programs are supplemented by mass vaccination campaigns.

Likewise, the effectiveness of anti-infective drugs is clearly demonstrated through prolonged life or better health in those infected with viral diseases such as AIDS, parasitic infections such as malaria, and bacterial infections such as tuberculosis and pneumococcal pneumonia.

But current research and development is not filling the pipeline for new anti-infective drugs as rapidly as resistance is developing, nor is vaccine development providing vaccines for some of the most common and lethal communicable diseases. At the same time, providing people with access to existing anti-infective drugs, vaccines, and goods such as condoms or bed nets—necessary for the control of communicable diseases in many developing countries—remains a great challenge.

Education, experimentation, and the discoveries that grow from them are the tools needed to combat high mortality infectious diseases, diseases that cause disability, or emerging and re-emerging infectious diseases. At the same time, partnerships between developing and industrialized countries can overcome many of the challenges of access to goods and technologies. This book may inspire its readers to set out on the path of drug and vaccine development, or on the path to discovering better public health technologies by applying our present understanding of the human genome and those of various infectious agents. Readers may likewise be inspired to help ensure wider access to those protective goods and technologies. Such inspiration, with pragmatic action, will keep us on the winning side of the struggle against communicable diseases.

David L. Heymann
Assistant Director General,
Health Security and Environment
Representative of the Director General for Polio Eradication
World Health Organization
Geneva, Switzerland

1
The History of Polio

It is likely that polio has caused paralysis and death for most of human history. One of the earliest written accounts of polio is that of the Pharaoh Siptah, who ruled ancient Egypt from 1200 B.C. to 1193 B.C. It is said that Siptah was stricken with a paralyzing **disease** as a young boy. The illness left his left foot and leg deformed. People of the time believed that Siptah was being punished for his father's sins because his father had overthrown the previous Pharaoh Seti II and seized the throne.

In addition to Siptah's story, the oldest identifiable reference to polio also comes from Egypt in the form of an Egyptian *stele*, a stone engraving that is more than 3,000 years old (Figure 1.1). The engraving depicts Ruma, a Syrian who served as a gatekeeper at the temple of Astarte in Egypt. When Ruma was five years old, he suffered from pain in his head and a sore leg. When his condition did not improve, his father took him to the temple to see the priest who, it was believed, would cure him with potions, charms, and amulets. The treatments did not work, and Ruma was left with a paralyzed right leg.

The stele explains that Ruma's leg withered as he got older and that he was forced to use the long stick shown in the engraving as a crutch. He is shown with his wife Ama and his young son Ptah-m-heb. Ruma is carrying fruit, wine, and a gazelle as gifts of thanks to the goddess he believes saved his life.

Sanitation was poor in ancient days, and therefore people were frequently exposed to sewage that contained bacteria and viruses, including the active poliovirus. In the case of poliovirus, the virus entered the sewage system because poliovirus passes through the intestines and into the feces of infected people, and the feces contaminated the water. Interestingly, this

Figure 1.1 Polio has plagued humans for thousands of years. Some of the earliest descriptive accounts of the disease come from ancient Egyptian steles, or stone engravings, like the one pictured above. This particular stele depicts the deformed foot of a man assumed to be Ruma of Syria. (Courtesy WHO)

presence in the sewage system also helped to create immunity, keeping cases at a much lower level than what would be seen after the development of sewage systems. When a person is frequently exposed to very low levels of a virus that are not sufficient to cause the disease, constant exposure stimulates the immune system into making antibodies against the virus, which will protect the individual.

Gradually people learned to dump waste away from the drinking water supply, a measure that protected against diseases like cholera and polio, which are often spread via contaminated water. However, low-level exposure no longer occurred, and thus people no longer developed immunity. The number of polio cases increased.

THE BIBLE SPEAKS OF POLIO

Many references to polio appear in the Bible. In the book of Luke 5:18 the reference to polio is translated using the word *palsy*: "And, behold, men brought in a bed a man which was taken with a palsy: and they sought means to bring him in, and to lay him before him."

In English language translations of the Bible, the word *palsy* is used instead of the word *paralysis* because it is derived from the Old French word *paralesie,* which actually means paralysis. Middle English shortened this into *palesie,* which appeared as *palsy* in the King James Version of the Bible in the seventeenth century. Of course, today we use the word *paralysis* when referring to the result of an infection with the poliovirus.

Another reference to polio appears in the book of Matthew 8:5–6 "And when Jesus was entered into Capernaum, there came unto him a centurion, beseeching him, and saying, Lord, my servant lieth at home sick of the palsy, grievously tormented."

Polio appears again in the Acts of the Apostles 9:33. Here the permanent paralysis associated with polio is described: "And there he found a certain man named Aeneas, which had kept his bed eight years, and was sick of the palsy."

Matthew 12:9–10 evokes the shriveling that often results when a person is stricken with polio: "Going on from that place, he went into their synagogue, and a man with a shriveled hand was there."

An additional reference to polio describing withering and the inability to walk due to that condition appears in John 5:2–3, 5: "Now there is at Jerusalem by the sheep market a pool, which is called in the Hebrew tongue Bethesda, having five porches. In these lay a great multitude of impotent folk, of blind, halt, withered, waiting for the moving of the water. And a certain man was there, which had an infirmity thirty and eight years."

A DISEASE OF CHILDREN
Polio generally afflicts the young. Although these biblical references do not specifically mention children, later historical accounts do. Sir Walter Scott (1771–1832), a Scottish novelist and poet, wrote about his own case of polio. His account, written in 1827, was the earliest recorded in the United Kingdom:

> I showed every sign of health and strength until I was about 18 months old. One night, I have been often told, I showed great reluctance to be caught and put to bed, and after being chased about the room, was apprehended and consigned to my dormitory with some difficulty. It was the last time I was to show much personal agility. In the morning I was discovered to be affected with the fever which often accompanies the cutting of large teeth. It held me for three days. On the fourth, when they went to bathe me as usual, they discovered that I had lost the power of my right leg . . . when the efforts of regular physicians had been exhausted, without the slightest success . . . the impatience of a child soon inclined me to struggle with my infirmity, and I began by degrees to stand, walk, and to run. Although the limb affected was much shrunk and contracted, my general health, which was of more importance, was much strengthened by

being frequently in the open air, and, in a word, I who in a city had probably been condemned to helpless and hopeless decrepitude, was now a healthy, high-spirited, and, my lameness apart, a sturdy child. [1]

In 1789, Michael Underwood, a British physician, published the first known clinical description of polio as a "Debility of the Lower Extremities." Once again, the passage refers to children:

> The disorder intended here is not noticed by any medical writer within the compass of my reading, or is not a common disorder, I believe, and it seems to occur seldomer in London than in some parts . . . It seems to arise from debility, and usually attacks children previously reduced by fever; seldom those under one, or more than four or five years old. The Palsy . . . sometimes seizes the upper, and sometimes the lower extremities; in some instances, it takes away the entire use of the limb, and in others, only weakens them." [2]

In analyzing the content of Underwood's description from a twenty-first-century point of view, anyone who is very familiar with polio can see that the description was technically accurate for a doctor of the eighteenth century. This is surprising since there was not much known about polio during this time. A twenty-first-century physician could have written the account. Because polio has historically occurred more often in children than in adults, the term *infantile paralysis* was originally used to identify the disease.

POLIO MAKES THE NEWS

Outbreaks of polio in Europe were not recorded until the early nineteenth century. In 1840, a German orthopedic surgeon named Jacob von Heine wrote the first detailed description

Figure 1.2 Sir Walter Scott is shown in this portrait with the cane he needed to walk. (© Bettmann/CORBIS)

of polio based on his studies of infected patients. His writings identified the spinal cord as the site of involvement, which we now know is correct.

Von Heine's description came only five years after small outbreaks of polio were reported in the United States and United Kingdom. Considering how little was known about polio during this period in history, von Heine's work was quite insightful and forward thinking. After his discovery, an interesting pattern developed. Polio **epidemics** in developed nations in the Northern Hemisphere began to be reported each summer and fall, but not in the spring or winter.

The epidemics became more and more severe, and the average age of those affected increased. The number of deaths from polio began to increase as well. A disease that had existed for thousands of years in only a few areas, and that had affected a limited number of people, was now coming to the forefront in many locations.

It was not until 1908 that the Viennese immunologist Karl Landsteiner and his associate Ervin Popper discovered that bacteria could not be found in the spinal cord tissue of infected humans. Perhaps, they thought, bacteria were not the cause of the disease. This led them to suggest that a virus was the causative agent of polio. Of course, without an electron microscope, they could not actually see the virus, but today we know that their supposition was correct.

DID YOU KNOW THAT . . .

Jacob von Heine published a 78-page monograph in 1840 that described the clinical features of polio and also noted that its symptoms suggested the involvement of the spinal cord. The limited medical knowledge of the time and the submicroscopic nature of the poliovirus kept von Heine and others from understanding the contagious nature of the disease. Even with the relatively large outbreaks of polio that occurred in Europe during the second half of the nineteenth century, physicians attributed the disease to causes such as teething, stomach upset, and trauma.

Figure 1.3 Karl Landsteiner was one of the first scientists to hypothesize that polio was a viral infection. Prior to his studies, researchers believed that bacteria caused the disease. Landsteiner and Ervin Popper proved their viral hypothesis by injecting spinal cord tissue from children who had died of polio into monkeys, which later developed the disease. (U.S. National Institutes of Health/National Library of Medicine)

A DYNAMIC EXPERIMENT

Landsteiner and Popper set out to test their hypothesis. To prove that a virus, not bacteria, was the cause of polio, they ground up the spinal cords of children who had died of polio and injected the material into monkeys. Soon the monkeys developed the disease.

The following year, researchers Simon Flexner and Paul Lewis, working at Johns Hopkins University in Baltimore, Maryland, confirmed Landsteiner and Popper's findings. This was of great importance since scientists could now attempt to find a vaccine to stop the spread of this deadly disease. Flexner and Lewis were able to successfully transfer polio from one monkey to another. They started out the same way that Landsteiner and Popper did, by injecting diseased human spinal cord tissue into the brains of monkeys. Once a monkey began to show symptoms, a suspension of its diseased spinal cord tissue was injected into other monkeys. Because each successive monkey developed the disease, their work was considered a huge success.

After the success of the experiment, Flexner was quoted as saying, "We failed utterly to discover bacteria, either in film preparations or in cultures, that could account for the disease." Therefore, they concluded, " . . . the infecting agent of epidemic poliomyelitis belongs to the class of the minute and filterable viruses that have not thus far been demonstrated with certainty under the microscope." [3]

HOW IS IT TRANSMITTED?

In the meantime, it became extremely important to find out how the disease was transmitted from one person to another. Initially, Flexner and Lewis felt that polio was spread directly from the nose to the brain. They introduced washings from the nose and throat of infected people into monkey nasal passages. Because the monkeys developed polio, the scientists concluded that this was the **mode of transmission**. For more than 20 years, people believed that this was, indeed, the way polio spread. Unfortunately, when scientists thought that this was the correct mode of transmission, they stopped searching for any other

Figure 1.4 Albert Sabin was the first researcher to show that the polio virus was present in the digestive system as well as the brain and spinal cord. Sabin developed the first oral vaccine for polio. Jonas Salk had earlier developed a polio vaccine that was given as an injection. (© AP Images)

mode of spreading the disease. Later it was found that this was not the route of transmission.

A hint as to the true means of spreading the disease was found in 1912, when Swedish researchers discovered poliovirus in the contents and walls of the human small intestine. At the time nobody knew that this was the real pathway of the virus. Unfortunately, because of Flexner and Lewis' work, it was believed that these intestinal viruses only existed because of swallowed nasal contents.

It was not until 1941 that a researcher named Albert Sabin (Figure 1.4) showed that poliovirus was not present in the nasal membranes of patients who had died. He was able to demonstrate the presence of the virus in the digestive tract as well as the brain and spinal cord. Other researchers were able to support Sabin's findings, and this led scientists to agree that polio actually began as a digestive illness.

Today we know that the majority of polio cases actually do not cause **symptoms** in those who are infected. In fact, symptoms only occur in approximately 5 percent of infections. One of three sets of symptoms occurs depending on which form of the disease a person actually has. The three forms of polio are mild polio, nonparalytic polio, and paralytic polio.

In a case of mild polio, a person will experience headache, nausea, vomiting, general discomfort, and a slight fever for about three days. These symptoms resemble a typical intestinal virus. Following this, the person will recover fully because the virus is defeated by the immune system before it can develop into anything more serious.

In a case of nonparalytic polio, the patient will have the same symptoms as with mild polio, with the addition of moderate fever, stiff back and neck, fatigue, and muscle pain. No paralysis occurs in this type of polio. It is sometimes referred to as **aseptic meningitis.**

Patients who actually develop paralytic polio will experience muscle weakness, stiffness, tremors, fever, constipation, muscle pain and **spasms**, and difficulty swallowing. These patients will most likely develop paralysis in one or both legs and/or arms. This paralysis can last days or weeks before strength returns. Some people will be permanently disabled. Depending on the degree of paralysis, their disabilities will vary.

2

The Transmission of Polio and How It Affects the Body

On the beautiful summer day of August 10, 1921, a 39-year-old lawyer named Franklin Delano Roosevelt (known familiarly to the public as FDR) was enjoying a well-earned vacation on Campobello Island in New Brunswick, Canada. Unfortunately, he had just lost the election of 1920 as the vice presidential candidate for the Democratic Party. However, the lost election did not put a damper on his spirits as he and his three eldest children, Anna, James, and Elliot, sailed around the island on his 24-foot sloop, *Vireo*.

After their trip, they returned home for a two-mile jog to their favorite pond for a swim. When the future president returned to the cottage, he felt a chill come over him and was too tired to eat with the family. He read for a while and went to bed with a sore back.

The next morning, he awoke with a fever of 102°F and aching, weak legs. As the day wore on, the pain in his legs spread to his back and neck, and eventually he was unable to move his legs at all. Until this point in his life he had been an active, healthy man who was used to exercising. He would spend the rest of his life in a wheelchair, never walking again (Figure 2.1).

What FDR did not know at first was that at some point in the weeks before he arrived at Campobello, he had contracted polio. The

Figure 2.1 Franklin Delano Roosevelt, who was president of the United States from 1933 until 1945, is one of the most famous survivors of polio. He had to use a wheelchair or strong leg braces due to the damage the disease had caused to his legs. (© AP Images)

usual incubation period for polio is 3 to 21 days, depending on how much virus the person is exposed to.

After several doctors examined Roosevelt and could not determine why he was not improving, they consulted Dr. Robert Lovett, a Harvard specialist and an expert on infantile paralysis. Sadly, he confirmed the family's worst fear: FDR had indeed contracted polio.

HOW DID THIS HAPPEN?

Naturally, everyone wanted to know: "How did he get sick in the first place?" It was known that the poliovirus could be transmitted through water, especially in the summer when people spent much time swimming, often in "water holes" that were contaminated by sewage. In an area where raw sewage is able to enter the water without first being treated, the poliovirus spreads easily. All a person has to do is swallow some of this contaminated water either from a drinking water supply or from a river, lake, or stream where he or she might be swimming. Once this happens, the virus infects the throat and intestinal tract.

Once in the cells of the intestinal tract, the virus **replicates**, or reproduces, making thousands of new viruses. These viruses are then carried through the intestinal tract and

DID YOU KNOW THAT . . .

Few Americans were ever aware of Franklin D. Roosevelt's disability. This was due in large part to the cooperation of members of the press who almost always photographed him from the waist up. FDR insisted on this policy when he re-entered politics after his bout with polio, and it was continued during his presidency. He felt that the nation should see him as a strong man with no physical problems. This would give the American people confidence in the government.

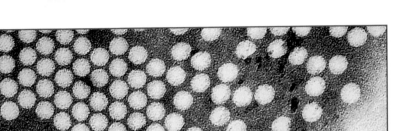

Figure 2.2 Polio is caused by the poliovirus. An electron micrograph of this virus is shown here. Poliovirus can cause symptoms ranging from mild discomfort and muscle weakness to total paralysis. Polio is usually spread through contaminated food and water. (CDC/Dr. Fred Murphy, Sylvia Whitfield)

released via the feces back into the sewage system to start the cycle all over again. In addition to spreading through untreated water, the virus can spread through human contact, especially among children who often do not wash their hands.

CATCHING THE BEAST

Viruses are not as complex as animal and plant cells, or even bacteria. They consist of only genetic material and a protein coat. They do not have any systems such as a digestive or reproductive system. In order to replicate, they require a living cell that they can invade so they may introduce their genetic information into the host. Poliovirus infects a person in the same way that other viruses cause infections. Humans are the only natural host for the virus (Figure 2.2).

When a virus enters the body, it seeks out cells that have specific proteins on their surface. These proteins are called receptor sites and act like parking spaces for the virus. As long as there is a place to park, the virus attaches to the cell and introduces its genetic information into the nucleus of the cell where all of the genes are located.

The viral genes become part of the host cell's genetic makeup and then direct the cell to act like a photocopier to produce millions of copies of the virus. The cell eventually bursts and releases the new viruses into the system so they can infect even more cells. Of course, when these cells burst, there is damage to the tissue.

HOW DOES IT WORK?

The initial poliovirus infection occurs in the intestinal tract. Once these cells are infected, one of several situations may occur. A person may be **asymptomatic**, meaning that he or she does not develop the disease or show any symptoms. Or he or she may have mild symptoms including a headache, fever, and vomiting that last for 72 hours or less.

If a person does develop symptoms, he or she may have a nonparalytic and less serious form of the disease. In such a case, the patient will suffer with diarrhea, a moderate fever, excessive fatigue, vomiting, pain, muscle tenderness, and spasms in any area of the body. These symptoms may last for up to two weeks and then disappear, leaving the patient with no further problems.

Approximately one percent of all polio patients develop the paralytic form of polio. These patients develop a stiff neck and back, fever, pain, and headaches. Muscle weakness can come on

Figure 2.3 Polio can affect the medulla oblongata, the part of the brain that controls breathing. If this happens, the patient may have trouble breathing or not be able to breathe at all without help. The iron lung, invented in 1928 by Philip Drinker, helps people who cannot breathe on their own. The machine encloses the patient from the neck down, forms an airtight seal, and regulates the pressure surrounding the patient's chest, thus aiding the breathing process. (CDC/GHO/Mary Hilpertshauser)

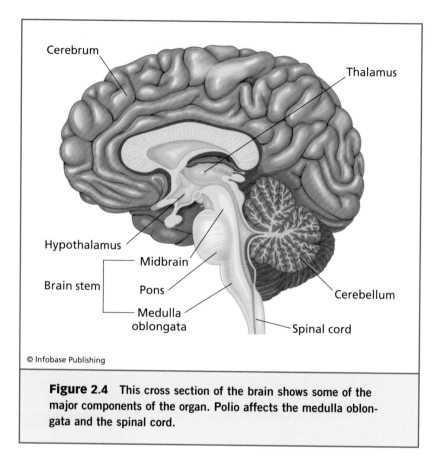

© Infobase Publishing

Figure 2.4 This cross section of the brain shows some of the major components of the organ. Polio affects the medulla oblongata and the spinal cord.

quickly anywhere in the body and may develop into paralysis. In the case of paralytic polio, the virus spreads through the bloodstream to infect cells located in the anterior portion of the spinal cord. This area is used to send signals to muscles so they can move. When these cells are destroyed, the muscles that used to receive signals from them in order to move can no longer function, and **paralysis** occurs. In addition, the person may have difficulty urinating and swallowing, muscle spasms, and trouble breathing. Up to 10 percent of these cases end in death.

If the virus affects the cells of the **medulla oblongata**, the structure that controls breathing, a person develops bulbar polio. In these cases, breathing becomes almost impossible without the aid of a device called an iron lung. This was developed by Philip Drinker and Louis Agassiz Shaw in 1928 and was used for several decades to help people with bulbar polio to breathe. The iron lung was a large metal machine that helped regulate the air pressure surrounding the patient's chest, thus allowing air to be pulled into the lungs of a person who could not breathe on his or her own. The patient was enclosed in the machine, from neck to toes, and an airtight seal was formed around the neck. Today, iron lungs are only occasionally used to help people breathe.

THE TREATMENT PLAN

Unfortunately, as with most viruses, there is no actual treatment that will cure a case of polio. That does not mean, however, that some of the patients suffering cannot find some relief. In addition to using a ventilator, if necessary, to aid breathing, a patient can be given medicines that reduce the headaches, muscle spasms, and pain. If a urinary tract infection develops, antibiotics are prescribed. Physical therapy and even surgery may prove useful to help restore some of the individual's lost muscle function.

Sister Elizabeth Kenny in Australia developed an interesting and useful form of therapy in 1933. She believed that the main problem in early polio cases was muscle spasms. She felt strongly that applying hot packs and using physical therapy was the best method to treat patients when they first developed the disease. This belief stemmed from her observation that Aboriginal children in Australia who had polio were treated with hot cloths.

During this time period, many doctors believed that **immobilization** using splints and casts was the best way to treat a polio victim. It is easy to see how a disagreement between Sister Kenny and the medical profession developed. In fact, one of her

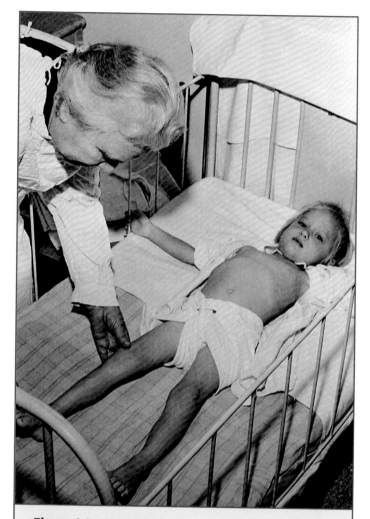

Figure 2.5 Sister Elizabeth Kenny, shown here with a young polio patient, believed that hot packs and massages would help polio patients regain use of their muscles, a method she developed in 1933. Although her methods were popular in her native Australia, doctors in the United States believed in immobilization of the afflicted limbs. Kenny's technique was finally accepted as an alternative therapy for polio when she was invited to become a guest faculty member at the University of Minnesota in 1940. (© Bettmann/CORBIS)

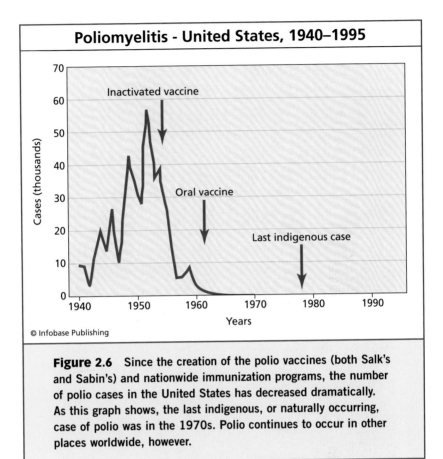

Figure 2.6   Since the creation of the polio vaccines (both Salk's and Sabin's) and nationwide immunization programs, the number of polio cases in the United States has decreased dramatically. As this graph shows, the last indigenous, or naturally occurring, case of polio was in the 1970s. Polio continues to occur in other places worldwide, however.

most outspoken critics was Dr. Robert Lovett, the polio special-ist who had treated Franklin D. Roosevelt in 1921.

Never losing her determination, Sister Kenny did not get angry. She opened the first polio treatment clinic in Townsville, Queensland, Australia, in 1933. Kenny persisted in her work and developed an attitude of understanding toward her critics:

The American doctor, in my opinion, possesses a com-bination of conservatism and that other quality which has put the United States in the forefront in almost every department of science—that is, an eagerness to know what it is really all about, in order that he may not be the one left behind if there is something to it. This eagerness, however, does not persuade him to abandon caution.[1]

Sister Kenny was well received at the University of Minnesota and became a guest faculty member there. Many medical doctors set aside their differences of opinion and accepted her treatment methods because she had a good success rate in helping patients achieve partial recoveries. In 1943, she met with President Roosevelt and received funding from the National Foundation for Infantile Paralysis to be used to train Kenny therapists at the University of Minnesota.

Today, in the United States, polio is considered a disease of the past. This is thanks to the extensive vaccination campaign that began with the development of the Salk vaccine in 1952 and later with the introduction of the Sabin oral **vaccine** in 1962. Both vaccines will be discussed in later chapters. In the Western Hemisphere, naturally occurring polio has not been seen since 1994.

3

Vaccines and How They Work

Most children don't like getting vaccinated. "Ouch," they may say. "That hurts!" In the end, though, it is worth the discomfort. It would be safe to say that the development of vaccinations is one of the most important contributions to the survival of mankind (Figure 3.1). They have helped to protect us, our pets, and our livestock from many different diseases. Along with advances in technology and medicine, vaccinations have helped to increase today's average human lifespan in the United States to approximately 77 to 80 years of age. That is not a bad achievement, considering that at the beginning of the twentieth century the average lifespan was only 47 years.

THE BODY'S ARMED FORCES

In order to understand how vaccinations work, we must review one of the human body's systems that helps us to stay healthy and free from disease. That system is known as the *immune system*. The immune system is complex and includes several organs, specialized cells in our blood, and different chemicals. All of these parts work together to fight off attacks by bacteria, viruses, parasites, and other invaders. This system might be considered the body's armed forces.

The skin acts as a general defender against invasion by physically blocking access to our bodies. When we get a cut or a scrape, the blocking ability of the skin is compromised, and we can get a localized infection due to invasion by **microorganisms**. It is at this point that other parts of the immune system go into action.

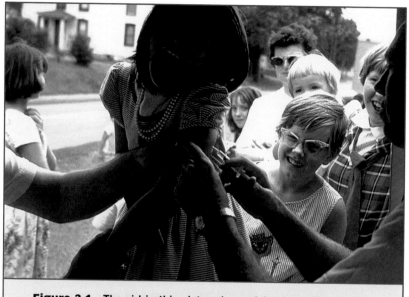

Figure 3.1 The girl in this picture is receiving her polio vaccine. A nationwide program of polio vaccination has virtually eliminated the virus in the United States. Two types of polio vaccine exist: the inactivated polio vaccine and the oral vaccine, which uses an attenuated virus. (Courtesy CDC)

Special cells known as white blood cells (also known as **leukocytes**) now begin to move into action. There are five different kinds of these cells that make up part of our immune system. Here we will focus on two types, **neutrophils** and **lymphocytes**.

One type of white blood cell, known as a neutrophil (Figure 3.2), is always found circulating in our blood. When the invasion occurs, special chemicals attract these cells to the site where the bacteria or other microorganisms have been allowed to enter. When they encounter the invaders, the neutrophils attack by engulfing and digesting them. This process is called **phagocytosis** (Figure 3.3). The neutrophil has a "cousin" called the **macrophage**. This cell also has the power to perform phagocytosis. Both cells are classified as phago-cytes. This actually means "eating cells" (from the Greek *phago*=eating, and the Latin *cyte*=cell).

Another type of white blood cell is the lymphocyte. Lymphocytes produce **antibodies**, which are small proteins that attach themselves onto the surface of the invaders. This helps the phagocytes to recognize and attack the micro-organisms. Along with antibodies that are attached to the surface of the invader, antibodies circulating in the blood-stream also help to fight **infections**.

The type of lymphocyte that produces antibodies is known as a B cell. B cells become activated by **antigens**, which are substances that the immune system recognizes as foreign to the

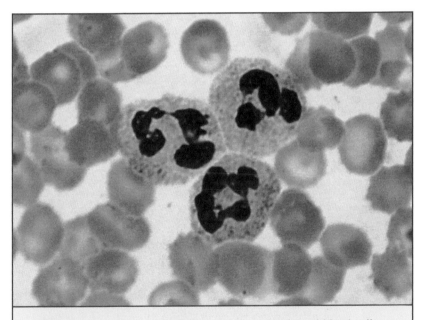

Figure 3.2 These neutrophils are surrounded by red blood cells. Neutrophils are the first leukocytes to arrive at the site of an inva-sion by microorganisms. They are the most abundant of white blood cells. (© Dr. Fred Hossler/Visuals Unlimited.)

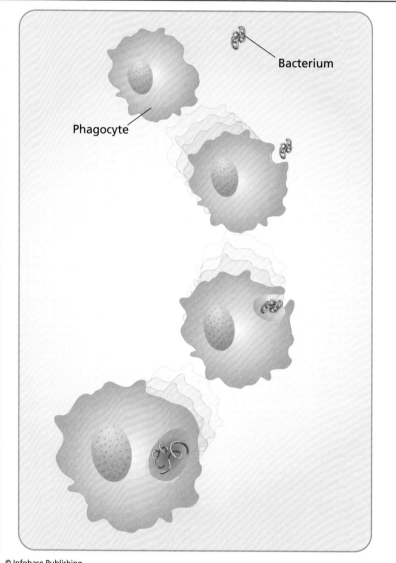

Figure 3.3   White blood cells act as the body's soldiers to protect it from harm. The phagocyte is one of these soldiers. When a phagocyte encounters a foreign particle, it will engulf the particle through a process called phagocytosis. The phagocyte reaches out its "arms," which surround the particle and pull it inside the phagocyte.

body. The surface proteins of bacteria, viruses, fungi, and other microorganisms can act as antigens because they are foreign to the body.

When a person comes down with a particular disease, such as poliomyelitis, the proteins on the surface of the virus are recognized by the immune system as foreign. The B cells are activated by the presence of the antigens (a process known as sensitization), convert to plasma cells, and produce antibodies that recognize the surface proteins of the virus. Once the B cell is sensitized, it may change to a plasma cell only when it gets a signal from another type of lymphocyte. This lymphocyte is called a helper T cell. Without the "OK" from the helper T cell, no antibodies will be produced.

When the B cells are introduced for the first time to the foreign antigens of the poliovirus, it will take some time for the body to produce the necessary antibodies to fight the invading organisms. This is known as the primary response. Unfortunately, during the time needed to produce the antibodies, the virus can incubate and cause disease.

Once a primary response occurs, the B cells are able to memorize the structure of the antigen for future reference. Should the body be exposed again to the same antigen, the B cells can swiftly make antibodies long before the organism has a chance to cause the disease. This antibody production caused by re-exposure to the antigen is called the secondary response. It is also known as the **anamnestic** response. This is where the vaccine enters the picture. Vaccinations initiate a low-level response by introducing a small amount, or a modified form, of the antigen into the body. This is not enough to cause the disease, but rather to stimulate the body to produce antibodies. Thus, the need for vaccinations is of utmost importance.

THE FIRST VACCINE

The concept behind the first vaccine was actually very simple. A method was needed to expose a person to a disease, have them make protective antibodies, and be sure they did not actually develop the disease. Of course, the concept may have been simple, but the difficult part was how to go about doing the work.

During the Song Dynasty in China (A.D. 960–1280), the Chinese people routinely practiced a procedure known as *variolation* in order to protect against smallpox. A person would place the powdered crusts of smallpox pustules into a scratch or inhale the dust. In most cases, the individual would develop a mild form of the disease and then become immune to smallpox for life. Unfortunately, some people would develop a true case of smallpox and die. However, this did not happen very often, so people were willing to undergo the procedure in order to be protected against the deadly disease.

Variolation continued to be used in China and the Middle East during this period, but did not appear in Europe until the early 1700s. When Lady Mary Wortley Montagu, the wife of the British ambassador to Turkey, immunized her children against smallpox using this method, it became popular in Europe. Unfortunately, people who underwent this procedure were contagious. In addition, the procedure was expensive and only the rich could afford to be variolated. These factors left most of the population unprotected.

Later, in 1796, the first vaccine that would eventually be recognized as safe was administered. At that time, a British physician named Edward Jenner wondered why milkmaids who had developed cowpox (a disease similar to smallpox but not as life threatening) did not develop small-pox. During this period in history, as in the past, smallpox was recognized as one of the worst diseases known to man. It often killed its victims, many of whom were infants and children.

Jenner compared the pox found on cows that had cow-pox to those on humans with smallpox. He realized that there was a great similarity between the two diseases and concluded that the milkmaids must have developed resistance to smallpox from their exposure to cowpox, which was a much milder disease. Today, we know that cowpox and smallpox viruses are both members of the orthopox virus family and that their DNA is very similar.

A DANGEROUS EXPERIMENT

In order to test his theory, Jenner performed a daring and dangerous experiment. On May 14, 1796, a milkmaid by the name of Sara Nelmes came to Jenner suffering from a case of cowpox. Jenner took a piece of metal, scratched several of her pox with it, and then transferred the material he had collected to James Phipps, his gardener's son (Figure 3.4). James soon developed cowpox.

On July 1, once James had recovered from cowpox, Jenner attempted to give him a case of smallpox. When James did not develop the disease, Jenner declared that the boy was successfully vaccinated. The word *vaccination* was derived from the Latin word *vacca*, meaning cow. To demonstrate his confidence in the vaccine, he then successfully vaccinated his own son.

In 1798, following his success, Jenner published his findings in a book entitled *An Inquiry into the Causes and Effects of the Variolæ Vaccinæ*. He spent the rest of his career studying the vaccination process, promoting it, and supplying physicians with cowpox material so they could also vaccinate people against smallpox. He summed up his dedication to the cause by saying, "I shall myself continue to prosecute this inquiry, encouraged by the pleasing hope of its becoming essentially beneficial to mankind."

Today there are many vaccines available to help protect us from diseases that were once devastating to mankind. They are delivered either by injection or by mouth, as is done with the Sabin vaccine against poliomyelitis. In the end, they

Figure 3.4 In a daring experiment, Edward Jenner deliberately exposed James Phipps to cowpox. After the boy recovered from the disease, which is a mild form of the disease smallpox, he was shown to be immune to smallpox. This painting depicts Jenner inoculating the boy with material from a cowpox pustule taken from a milkmaid. Jenner's experiment paved the way for vaccine research. (Sisters)

all work in the same way. Their purpose is to stimulate the immune system to produce antibodies and to keep a memory of the foreign invader or toxin that could cause a disease.

With this memory, if the body is exposed to the real disease organisms or toxins, the immediate production of antibodies will take place and protect us.

MAKING THE VACCINE

In order to make the vaccine, the organism (such as the poliovirus) or a toxin made by an organism (such as that seen in a case of **tetanus**) must be either weakened or destroyed, a process called *attenuation*. One way this can be done is by cooling the tissue culture in which the virus is grown, thus creating a virus that grows slowly at body temperature. The organism can also be treated with special chemicals, such as aluminum salts when we want to make a tetanus **toxoid** vaccine, or **formaldehyde** for making other vaccines.

Two scientists, Jonas Salk and Albert Sabin, worked independently to create a polio vaccine. The Salk polio vaccine was created by killing the virus with formaldehyde and then purifying the mixture to collect the dead virus. Sabin used a live, **attenuated**, or weakened, virus in his vaccine. In this type of vaccine, the virus is grown in culture at lower than normal temperatures. Over time, a strain of virus that can exist at these lower temperatures develops. When purified and collected, the virus can infect human

DID YOU KNOW THAT . . .

In light of the recent attention to bioterrorism, many people have voiced concerns about the possibility that terrorists might use the smallpox virus as a weapon. Because smallpox as a disease has been eradicated from the face of the Earth, doctors have not been giving vaccinations for many years. The government of the United States has assured its people that there is sufficient smallpox vaccine in storage to vaccinate the entire population of the United States if necessary.

cells, but only very slowly because it is now used to growing at colder than body temperature. The slow development of the virus in the vaccinated individual allows the immune system to create antibodies before a true case of the disease can make the person ill. This technique is also used to create the measles vaccine. The work of Salk and Sabin will be described in more detail in Chapters 4 and 5.

Another type of vaccine is called the **subunit vaccine**. This is made by isolating the antigens or parts of the antigens of the infectious organism and introducing these to the patient. Today vaccines made in this way are used to fight against meningitis, pneumonia, whooping cough (also known as pertussis), and a serious childhood respiratory disease caused by the bacterium *Haemophilus influenzae* type b.

Table 3.1   Examples of Different Types of Vaccines

Vaccine Type	Representative Examples
Live Attenuated	Measles, Mumps, Rubella (MMR) Oral Polio (Sabin) Varicella (chicken pox) Intranasal Influenza
Killed (Inactivated)	Injectable Polio (Salk) Influenza
Toxoid	Diphtheria (alone or in combination with Tetanus or with Pertussis and Tetanus) Tetanus (alone or in combination with Tetanus or with Pertussis and Tetanus)
Component (containing parts of the whole bacteria or virus)	*Haemophilus influenzae* (Hib) Hepatitis A (Hep A) Hepatitis B (Hep B) HPV Meningococcal meningitis Pneumococcal conjugate

Modern technological advances have led to the development of recombinant vaccines. These are made by taking the actual genes for a part of the viral protein coat and putting them into yeast cells, which then go on to produce the protein for the viral coat. The proteins are then injected into the patient, thus causing antibody production. This is a safe means of vaccinating an individual because the protein contains no viral DNA or RNA and, therefore, cannot infect a cell. However, it will bring about the production of antibodies to the viral coat protein. In addition to this technique, genetically engineered bacteria have been used to create safe vaccines in experimental trials. Gardasil®, the vaccine recently developed to protect against several strains of the human papillomavirus (HPV), is an example of a recombinant vaccine.

Conjugate vaccines are created by linking purified polysaccharides (complex sugars) from the coat of a disease-causing bacterium to a carrier protein. The polysaccharide is then recognized by the immune system as if it were a protein antigen. This type of vaccine has been used with great success in the United States to combat pneumococcal disease and meningococcal meningitis A.

Work is being done to create a number of important vaccines to be used worldwide against many diseases, including malaria, which kills several million people each year. In fact, the World Health Organization Initiative for Vaccine Research (IVR) was created in 2001 to expedite the development of vaccines against infectious diseases of major public health importance. In addition to this, the IVR is working to improve existing immunization technologies and to ensure that any advances made become available to the many people who need them most.

4

The Life of Jonas Salk

In New York City on October 28, 1914, a baby was born who would eventually change the condition of humanity forever. It was on this day that Jonas Edward Salk became the first child of Jewish-Russian immigrant parents. His father was a garment worker and his mother worked hard to make sure that her children received a good education and became successful (Figure 4.1).

Salk was the first in his family to attend college. While at the City University of New York, his initial desire was to become a lawyer. In fact, as a child he was not interested in the sciences. After a short time in college, however, his interests changed and he decided to pursue a career in medicine. Salk has said that part of this change in careers might have been due to his mother: "My mother didn't think I would make a very good lawyer. And I believe that her reasons were that I really couldn't win an argument with her."

A RESEARCH CAREER BEGINS

Following college, Salk entered New York University School of Medicine. At the end of his first year, he was asked to meet with a professor of chemistry, Dr. R. Keith Cannon. Salk was sure that he would be told he was failing or had done something wrong. Instead, Dr. Cannon offered him the opportunity to postpone medical school for one year in order to conduct chemistry research. Salk had always wanted to do research, so he took Cannon up on his offer.

Jonas Salk graduated from medical school in 1938. At that time he began to work with a **microbiologist** named Thomas Francis Jr. Dr. Francis had spent years studying **influenza**. When Salk began to work with him, they spent a long time creating a vaccine for it.

Figure 4.1 Jonas Salk, inventor of the first polio vaccine, examines test tubes in his laboratory at the University of Pittsburgh. After eight years of research, he created a vaccine using an inactivated form of the polio virus. The vaccine was given to the public beginning April 12, 1955. (© Bettmann/CORBIS)

This dreaded disease had killed millions of people during World War I, and scientists hoped to find a vaccine to avoid another devastating outbreak. Salk and Francis were successful and created a vaccine in 1942 that was used by armed forces personnel during World War II.

In 1947, Salk began research at the University of Pittsburgh Medical School. The National Foundation for Infantile Paralysis, aware of his success with the influenza vaccine, wanted him to work with them on a vaccine for polio. He spent the next eight years creating such a vaccine. Salk's dedication to his work may easily be seen in the following quotation from a 1991 interview in San Diego, California:

> We were told in one lecture that it was possible to immunize against diphtheria and tetanus by the use of chemically treated toxins, or toxoids. And the following lecture, we were told that for immunization against a virus disease, you have to experience the infection, and that you could not induce immunity with the so-called "killed" or inactivated, chemically treated virus preparation. Well, somehow, that struck me. What struck me was that both statements couldn't be true. And I asked why this was so, and the answer that was given was in a sense, "Because." There was no satisfactory answer.[1]

DID YOU KNOW THAT . . .

Although the Salk vaccine was a huge success, initially there was a problem with the vaccine. The vaccine actually induced 260 cases of poliomyelitis, including 10 deaths. The problem was traced to incomplete inactivation of some virus particles, which was soon corrected. Since then the vaccine has been highly effective, with a 70–90 percent protection rate.[2]

Salk was a man who did not believe in following others. He was always thinking, challenging, and creating. Hard work did not daunt him.

During the same interview, Salk said that he was curious, even as a young child:

> There was a photograph of me when I was a year old, and there was that look of curiosity on that infant's face that is inescapable. I have the suspicion that this curiosity was very much a part of my early life: asking questions about unreasonableness. I tended to observe, and reflect and wonder. That sense of wonder, I think, is built into us.

SWEET SUCCESS

On July 2, 1952, Salk used a refined vaccine on children who had already suffered from a case of polio and recovered. Once vaccinated, the antibody levels in their blood increased. Following this, he tried his vaccine on volunteers who had never been exposed to polio. This included his wife, children, and himself. Once again, antibodies were produced and nobody became ill.

This was very encouraging to Salk. In fact, he would later say that the experience was "the thrill of my life. Compared to the feeling I got looking under the microscope, everything that followed was anticlimactic." The governmental leaders were also very proud and wanted the world to know that Salk's success was achieved in Pittsburgh. Much publicity followed in an effort to show that the city was a major center of medical care and research.

In 1953, Dr. Francis designed, supervised, and evaluated field trials of the polio vaccine that Salk had developed. He used a double-blind statistical analysis where neither the patients nor the participating physicians knew if an inoculation was a placebo (an inert substance used as an experimental control) or the real vaccine. Approximately 1.8 million children from the United States, Canada, and Finland participated in the trial.

In 1955, after much hard work and dedication, Jonas Salk was successful in releasing the first vaccine effective against the dreaded poliovirus. On April 12, 1955, news of the creation of the vaccine was released to the public. Millions breathed a sigh of relief in the knowledge that finally one of the great scourges of mankind would be defeated. In addition to this, Salk was hailed as a hero, not only for his success, but also for his refusal to patent his discovery. He did not care whether or not he would become rich from it; he merely wanted the vaccine to be available to as many people as possible.

Salk made his vaccine from "killed" virus that he treated with formaldehyde. The treatment rendered the virus completely unable to cause polio. This is in contrast to Albert Sabin's technique, which used a weakened, or attenuated, virus that could still cause polio in someone with a weakened immune system.

Although the virus was no longer able to cause a case of polio, it was still capable of bringing about an immune response that would protect an individual if he or she were exposed to the live virus.

THE SALK INSTITUTE OPENS

In 1963, Salk opened the Jonas Salk Institute for Biological Studies in La Jolla, California. The National Science Foundation and the March of Dimes were instrumental in the funding of the research center. Salk's problem had been in deciding where to open the institute. In 1960, Charles Dail, the mayor of San Diego, offered Salk 70 acres of land right next to the University of California at San Diego. He took the offer and the rest is history. Incidentally, Mayor Dail was himself a victim of polio.

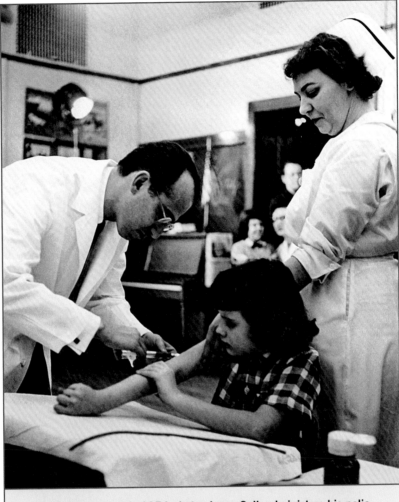

Figure 4.2 In this 1954 photo, Jonas Salk administers his polio vaccine to a young girl. The polio vaccine went through extensive field testing before it was released to the general public in 1955. (© Bettmann/CORBIS)

After his phenomenal success with the polio vaccine, Salk did not rest. He spent several years writing. In 1972, he released *Man Unfolding*, a book that focused on the pattern of order in living things. In 1973, he published *The Survival of the Wisest,* which stressed that man will survive if he makes judgments in advance rather than after he has acted on something. Salk went on to publish *World Population and Human Values: A New Reality,* in 1981. This book looked at the changing values of society as the world population increased. In 1983, he wrote *Anatomy of Reality,* in which he stated, "The most meaningful activity in which a human being can be engaged is one that is directly related to human evolution."

Salk's last years were devoted to work on finding a vaccine for the world's new dreaded disease, AIDS. Unfortunately, he never succeeded as he had with his polio vaccine. Jonas Salk died of congestive heart failure on June 23, 1995. His legacy will live on forever.

5

The Life of Albert Sabin

On August 26, 1906, in Bialystok, Poland, Tillie and Jacob Sabin became the proud parents of a son named Albert. He grew up in his native land until 1921 when, due to the spread of anti-Semitism, his parents decided it would be wise to emmigrate to the United States.

The family settled in Paterson, New Jersey, and Albert's father entered the silk and manufacturing business. Albert spoke no English when he first immigrated, but he learned quickly. Two years after arriving in the United States, Albert entered New York University. In 1924, only one year after his admission, he earned a bachelor of arts degree. He continued his education until 1926 at the NYU College of Dentistry. He received his bachelor of science degree in 1927.

Sabin was clearly a brilliant student. He furthered his studies by entering the NYU Medical College in 1927 (the same college from which Jonas Salk graduated) and graduated in 1931. He went on to become the house physician at Bellevue Hospital in New York. Then, in 1934, he received a National Research Council fellowship at the Lister Institute in London, England.

Sabin continued his work in London for only one year. He returned to New York to work as a research assistant at the prestigious Rockefeller Institute for Medical Research. His research interests at the institute included work with viruses and the immune system. He had success in cultivating the rabies virus in the laboratory and creating a better rabies vaccine for dogs. He also worked with pneumonia and polio.

Albert Sabin was responsible for discovering the true nature of the poliovirus. Originally it was believed that the virus was a member of the herpesvirus family. Sabin proved that it was a newly discovered virus in a family not previously identified (picornavirus). He also showed how poliovirus entered the body. It had been believed that the mode of entry was through the nasal membranes. Sabin showed that the virus entered more often through the digestive system.

In 1939, Sabin became an associate professor at the Children's Hospital Research Foundation at the University of Cincinnati in Ohio. Thanks to his efforts, a department of virology and microbiology was established there.

Sabin served in the United States Army during World War II. He worked for the Army's Board for the Investigation of Epidemic Diseases. While there, he focused his research on sandfly fever virus and dengue fever virus. After World War II, he concentrated his efforts on polio research.

IN SEARCH OF A WEAK VIRUS

While reviewing data on the incidence of polio outbreaks, Sabin noticed that cases of polio were rare in areas of poor sanitation. Studies of antibody presence in children who lived in these areas showed that most of the children did, indeed, have antibodies to polio, but had never shown any symptoms of the disease. Sabin believed that these children had either been exposed to polio very early in life, when they still had antibodies from their mothers, or had been infected by weak strains of the virus that caused the production of antibodies without any symptoms.

Sabin began a quest to locate these weak viruses and traveled around the world in an effort to do so. He found three strains and began his work on an oral polio vaccine. The most frequently occurring strain of poliovirus is Strain I, also known as "Brunhilde." The other strains are Strain II (Lansing) and Strain III (Leon). Type 1 polio is the most common cause of epidemics and is associated with paralytic cases of the disease. Type 2 is the least common and is associated with a flulike illness that is not always accompanied by paralysis.

Worldwide, wild-type 2 virus has been virtually eliminated. The rate of occurrence of Type 3 virus falls between the other two. This type is associated with gastrointestinal symptoms and may also be accompanied by paralysis. Sabin intended for the vaccine to be delivered orally in a syrup form or on a sugar cube.

EUREKA!

After much work and dedication, Sabin met with success. The World Health Organization (WHO) felt so confident about the effectiveness of the vaccine, that it ordered testing on a worldwide basis. In 1954, Sabin tested the vaccine on himself and his two daughters. In 1957, Sabin was invited to be involved with the administration of the vaccine in Mexico, Chile, Sweden, Japan, Holland, and the Soviet Union. Sabin, like Salk, did not patent his vaccine and did not profit from its discovery.

Unfortunately, Sabin's success did not meet with the same acceptance in the United States as in other countries. Although an oral vaccine using attenuated virus would be more effective than an injected vaccine using killed virus, scientists believed that there was no better vaccine than the one developed by Jonas Salk. Testing and acceptance of Sabin's vaccine was delayed.

Sabin's oral vaccine had definite advantages over Salk's. The most obvious was that it did not require an injection. Children were much less afraid of taking the vaccine. Secondly, because Sabin's vaccine used live attenuated, or weakened, virus instead of the killed virus used by Salk, it brought about mucosal immunity in the intestinal tract where the virus first established itself. This would cause the destruction of the virus at the site of infection and not allow the virus to be spread through fecal contamination. Humoral, antibody-based immunity, also developed from this mode of viral introduction.

The most serious disadvantage of Sabin's oral vaccine is the risk of vaccine-associated paralytic polio (VAPP). This may

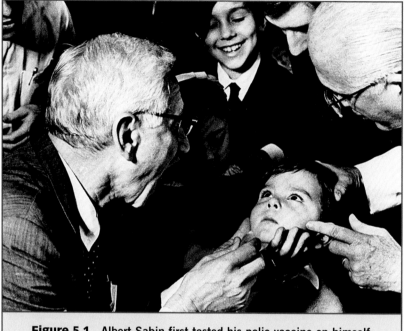

Figure 5.1 Albert Sabin first tested his polio vaccine on himself and his two daughters. Sabin is shown here giving his oral vaccine to five-year-old Luiz Inacio Gama. (© Bettmann/CORBIS)

develop because live viruses are used to prepare the vaccine. There is always the possibility that the attenuated form of the virus might revert back to a virulent form and bring about disease. Studies have shown that live viruses are shed in the stool for up to six weeks after vaccination. It has been estimated by the Centers for Disease Control and Prevention that worldwide one person per 2.5 million people receiving oral vaccine develops an active case of vaccine-associated paralytic polio. This, of course, would only occur in an individual who was not previously vaccinated. In the year 2000, a policy of using only inactivated polio vaccine (Salk vaccine) was adopted in the United States to avoid VAPP.

In Third World countries, other, highly prevalent gastrointestinal viruses interfere with the ability of the poliovirus to replicate in the patient's intestine, thus interfering with his or her ability to develop antibodies. Additionally, both vaccines require several boosters to induce protective immunity, so patient compliance plays an important role. Studies have revealed that in Third World countries 20 percent of people do not return for follow-up boosters.

One of the problems with the Salk vaccine was that it was injected; it did not expose intestinal cells to the virus, and only humoral immunity was created. This meant that although a person vaccinated with the Salk vaccine was

DID YOU KNOW THAT . . .

The World Health Organization has been keeping a close watch on the occurrence of polio cases worldwide. This shows where the hotspots have been located from February 2008 through August 2008.

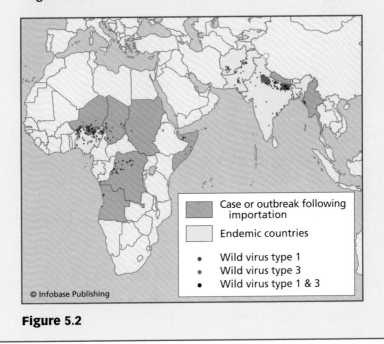

© Infobase Publishing

Case or outbreak following importation

Endemic countries

• Wild virus type 1
• Wild virus type 3
• Wild virus type 1 & 3

Figure 5.2

protected against polio, he or she could still be a **carrier** of the disease in his or her intestinal tract if he or she was exposed to a wild form of the virus.

SABIN SUNDAY

On April 24, 1960, the first test of Sabin's vaccine was held in the United States. Approximately 200,000 people lined up at numerous locations to receive vaccine. The day was referred to as "Sabin Sunday" and was a momentous occasion for the new vaccine and its creator. It was followed by two more "Sabin Sundays." By this time, 80 million people throughout the world had already been vaccinated. In 1970, Sabin received the National Medal of Science from President Richard Nixon. The president awarded the medal "for the vaccine that has eliminated poliomyelitis as a major threat to human health."

That same year, Sabin left Cincinnati to settle in Israel, where he became the president of the Weizmann Institute of Science. He remained in that position for two years before he had to step down to undergo open-heart surgery. After his recovery, he dedicated himself to research on cancer and a spray vaccine for measles.

In the early 1980s, Sabin was stricken with a disease that caused temporary paralysis. The condition, known as Guillain-Barré syndrome, is not related to polio in any way. It is usually the result of recovering from the flu or other respiratory illnesses and is often not a permanent problem. Following his recovery, Sabin became the senior consultant to the AIDS researchers at the National Institutes of Health in Bethesda, Maryland.

THE PRESIDENTIAL MEDAL OF FREEDOM

On May 12, 1986, Sabin received the Presidential Medal of Freedom from President Ronald Reagan. This is the highest award given to a civilian. In that same year, the city of

Figure 5.3 The Sabin oral polio vaccine was quite a success. On the first day the vaccine was offered, 200,000 people across the United States chose to receive it. Due to the large turnout, the day was called "Sabin Sunday." In the photo above, people line up at a Georgia grocery store to receive the vaccine. (Courtesy CDC/Charles N. Farmer)

Cincinnati renamed its newly expanded convention center after Albert Sabin.

Albert Sabin died in 1993 at the age of 86. It was estimated, at that time, that his vaccine had prevented nearly 5 million cases of polio. In addition, it probably helped 500,000 people worldwide avoid death from the once-dreaded disease.

THE PRESIDENTIAL MEDAL OF FREEDOM

The following is a partial transcript of the ceremony on May 12, 1986, when Albert Sabin, along with six other individuals, received the Presidential Medal of Freedom from President Ronald Reagan. The following is a portion of the president's speech:

Well, thank you all for being here. Nancy and I want to welcome you all to the White House for this happy occasion. On days like this and at lunches like this, I find myself looking up and thinking what a wonderful job I have. We're here today to present the Medal of Freedom to seven Americans. This medal is the highest civilian honor our nation can bestow. And I've always thought it highly significant that we call it not the Medal of Talent or the Medal of Valor or the Medal of Courage or Genius but the Medal of Freedom. I think that says a lot about our values and what we honor and what we love.

. . . You're all originals. You've all made America better—a better place—and you've made it seem a better place in the eyes of the people of the world. And this today is just our way of saying thanks. And without further ado, I'm going to read the citations for the medals now and award them to the recipients.

. . . When, as a boy, Albert Bruce Sabin came to the United States . . . no one could have known that he would number among the most prominent immigrants of our century. From an early age Sabin devoted his life to medicine, and by the 1950s his research had resulted in a breakthrough. In the years since, the Sabin vaccine has helped to make dramatic advances against the scourge of poliomyelitis.

This medal is awarded to Dr. Sabin on behalf of a proud nation and a grateful world. Doctor, thank you for everything.

There's nothing to add to achievements such as these, and no praise that can add any more luster to these great names. May I say to you simply, to all of you, thank you just for being, for doing what you've done and what you do. And thank you all, and God bless you.[1]

6

Nobody Is Exempt

Viruses and bacteria are usually not picky about what type of people they infect. They do not care, for example, whether a person is rich or poor. No matter what walk of life a person comes from, he or she is still quite able to catch any number of diseases and possibly die from them.

This has been the case with polio. Many rich and famous people were unable to escape it. Consider Franklin Delano Roosevelt. His experience with the disease was explained in Chapter 2. He may have gone on to become a president, but his life was permanently changed by polio.

Many other famous people, both men and women, have been stricken with polio. Some were athletes, some actors, and others musicians. They often contracted the disease in their childhood, and in some cases it left a lasting mark. However, the consequences of the disease did not stop them from achieving what they set out to do.

ALAN ALDA

On January 28, 1936, Alphonso D'Abruzzo was born in New York City to Robert Alda and Joan Brown. Robert was an actor and Joan was a former Miss New York pageant winner. In 1943, at the age of seven, Alphonso, later to be known as the famous actor Alan Alda (Figure 6.1), developed polio. He was confined to his bed for two years.

Thanks to his mother's efforts and her knowledge of the work of Sister Elizabeth Kenny, Alda was able to overcome his disease with no lasting problems. His mother used Kenny's technique of bandaging, massaging, and applying hot packs to his legs. He did not forget his two years of therapy, as can be seen by the following passage:

Figure 6.1 Many famous people have suffered from polio. Alan Alda, who starred in the hit television series *M*A*S*H*, suffered from the debilitating disease. Although he was confined to his bed for two years as a young boy, his mother used the techniques pioneered by Sister Kenny, and Alda fully recovered. (© AP Images)

The massages were extremely painful. It was a little bit like taking your thumb and bending it back to your elbow. To this day I'm not interested in getting a massage. People think it's wonderful. Not me. It's torture.[1]

Nevertheless, Alda was able to develop normally and went on to become one of the most famous television and movie actors today. His list of television and theatrical movies is long and impressive. Of course, his most famous role is probably that of Captain Benjamin Franklin "Hawkeye" Pierce on the television series *M*A*S*H*.

EMPEROR CLAUDIUS

Another famous person who suffered from polio lived in a different period of history, in a different land, and under very different circumstances. Claudius, Emperor of Rome, lived from 10 B.C. to A.D. 54. He was born Tiberius Claudius Drusus to Drusus Claudius Nero and his wife Antonia Minor, who was a daughter of Mark Antony.

Claudius suffered from a very serious limp, probably due to polio, and was constantly ill. Because he was eventually supposed to ascend the throne of Rome and was clearly disabled, he was kept out of sight for most of his childhood. Due to his disabilities, his parents considered him to be mentally infirm and therefore an embarrassment. Claudius spent most of his childhood in complete seclusion. However, he was not the unintelligent person that his family assumed him to be. Because he had a lot of free time on his hands, he read many books and became very knowledgeable. It was not until he was 46 years old that he held his first public office as a consul.

Through a series of events that included assassinations and overthrows, Claudius became Emperor of Rome on January 25, A.D. 41. His polio did not shorten his lifespan. Unfortunately, he was assassinated on October 13, A.D. 54.

WILMA RUDOLPH

Who could have ever imagined that a young girl who suffered from polio would one day become an Olympic medal winner for track and field? Despite her illness, Wilma Rudolph achieved this goal.

Figure 6.2 Wilma Rudolph contracted polio at the age of six and had to wear leg braces to help her walk. That did not stop her from being active. She was finally able to walk without braces and, at the age of 16, won the bronze medal at the 1960 Summer Olympics in Rome, Italy. (© AP Images)

Wilma was born in Tennessee on June 23, 1940, to Ed and Blanche Rudolph, poor but honest, hard-working people. She was the twentieth of 22 children. Wilma was born prematurely and weighed only four-and-one-half pounds. Because the family was poor, they could not afford good health care. In addition, due to segregation in the South, she was not allowed to be treated in the local, whites-only hospital. So her mother treated her at home for several illnesses, including scarlet fever and pneumonia.

When Wilma was six, her mother noticed that her left leg and foot were becoming deformed. When doctors examined her, they told her mother that Wilma would never walk again. However, Blanche Rudolph was not one to give up easily. She found out that Wilma could be treated at Meharry Hospital, located about 50 miles away. They made the journey, and the doctors fitted Wilma with leg braces. "I spent most of my time trying to figure out how to get them off," she said. "But when you come from a large, wonderful family, there's always a way to achieve your goals."

With help and support from her entire family, Wilma was able to remove her leg braces by the age of nine. After this, she became an avid basketball player. She spent a good deal of time playing basketball and eventually found that she was an excellent runner.

In 1956, at the age of 16, Rudolph competed in her first Olympic games and won a bronze medal in the 4x4 relay. At the Rome Olympics, on September 7, 1960, she was the first American woman to win three gold medals. She won for the 100-meter dash, the 200-meter dash, and as the anchor in the 400-meter relay. In 1983, she was elected to the United States Olympic Hall of Fame.

After retiring from competition, Wilma became a track coach at Burt High School in Clarksville, Tennessee. Later she coached in Maine and Indiana and became a sports commentator on national television. On November 12, 1994, she died at the age of 54 of brain cancer at her home in Nashville, Tennessee.

ITZHAK PERLMAN

Born on August 31, 1945, in Tel Aviv, Israel, Itzhak Perlman was unfortunate enough to contract polio at the age of four. This caused him to lose the use of his legs. But it did not stop him from becoming one of the most celebrated violinists in history. Although he is permanently disabled by his condition and must continue to use leg braces and crutches to get around, Perlman is a world-renowned muscian who loves to share his talent with others. He has even appeared on *Sesame Street.*

Perlman's dedication to his craft was described in an article that appeared in the *Houston Chronicle.* A description of how hard it is for him to negotiate the stage makes it clear just how much he loves his music and does not let having had polio interfere with his ability to perform.

> On Nov. 18, 1995, Itzhak Perlman, the violinist, came on stage to give a concert at Avery Fisher Hall at Lincoln Center in New York City. If you have ever been to a Perlman concert, you know that getting on stage is no small achievement for him.
>
> To see him walk across the stage one step at a time, painfully and slowly, is an unforgettable sight. He walks painfully, yet majestically, until he reaches his chair. Then he sits down, slowly, puts his crutches on the floor, undoes the clasps on his legs, tucks one foot back and extends the other foot forward. Then he bends down and picks up the violin, puts it under his chin, nods to the conductor and proceeds to play.
>
> By now, the audience is used to this ritual. They sit quietly while he makes his way across the stage to his chair. They remain reverently silent while he undoes the clasps on his legs. They wait until he is ready to play.[2]

Perlman began his training at the Tel Aviv Schulamit Academy shortly after contracting polio. By the time he was 10 years old, he was performing concerts with the Israel Broadcasting Orchestra. His family moved to New York where he attended the prestigious Juilliard School of Music. In 1964, he won the highly acclaimed Leventritt Competition. This was the key that opened

Figure 6.3 Itzhak Perlman cannot walk without crutches as a result of suffering from polio as a young boy. He is a world-renowned violinist. (© AP Images)

the door to a career that now includes hundreds of performances, recordings, television appearances, and awards.

In Itzhak Perlman's case, polio may have left him with a permanent disability that does not allow him to walk easily, but

DID YOU KNOW THAT . . .

Some famous people from all walks of life have suffered from polio. Here are just a few:

Ann Adams (1937–1992): artist, used her mouth to paint

Alan Alda (1936–): television star

Arthur C. Clarke (1917–2008): author

Claudius: Emperor of Rome (10 B.C.–A.D. 54)

Georgia Coleman (1912–1940): Olympic diver

CeDell Davis (1927–): jazz guitarist

Ian Dury (1942–2000): British rock star

Ray Ewry (1873–1937): Olympic track-and-field champion

Mia Farrow (1945–): actress

Henry Holden (1948–): actor, comedian, athlete, activist

Marjorie Lawrence (1907–1979): world-famous opera singer

Joni Mitchell (1943–): singer

Jack Nicklaus (1940–): golfer

Itzhak Perlman (1945–): internationally acclaimed violinist

Franklin Delano Roosevelt (1882–1945): United States president

Wilma Rudolph (1940–1994): athlete, Olympic gold medalist

Ruma: ancient Syrian

Siptah: Egyptian Pharaoh (fl. 1200 B.C.)

it surely did not stop him from achieving a level of success that most people only dream about.

DINAH SHORE

Frances "Fanny" Rose Shore was born in Winchester, Tennessee, on February 29, 1916. She was a healthy little girl until, at 18 months of age, she was stricken with polio. Fortunately, she received the Sister Kenny treatment from her parents and made a full recovery. She was left with only a slightly deformed foot and a mild limp, neither of which interfered with her ability to function normally.

Shore's response to treatment was so successful that she went on to become a high school cheerleader, graduated from Vanderbilt University in 1938, and, later in life, became a famous actress and singer. In many of her auditions, she sang the popular song "Dinah." Eventually, she was referred to by this name.

MARJORIE LAWRENCE

On February 17, 1907, Marjorie Lawrence was born in Deans Marsh, Victoria, Australia. She was a very athletic child. As a teenager she won several vocal competitions, and, in 1932, she debuted at the Metropolitan Opera in New York City as Brünnhilde in Richard Wagner's *Die Walküre*.

While on tour in Mexico in 1941, Lawrence began to have difficulty standing. Her symptoms worsened and she was diagnosed with polio. As a result of the disease, she was left in a wheelchair, unable to perform on the stage. In an effort to continue in the theater, she performed, seated in a chair, at charity concerts in Australia during World War II. Finding this extremely difficult, she left the stage, became a teacher, and eventually retired to her ranch, Harmony Hills, in Hot Springs, Arkansas, an area known for its famous hot springs. Lawrence knew that the waters would help to alleviate some of her pain. She continued to teach international students until her death in 1979.

FRANCIS FORD COPPOLA

When you think of the famous Godfather films, you can't help but remember the name Francis Ford Coppola. The famous director of those films, and many others, is another of the noteworthy people who have suffered from polio.

Figure 6.4 Director Francis Ford Coppola developed a love of movies and moviemaking while confined to bed at age nine with a case of polio. (© AP Images)

"When I was nine I was confined to a room for over a year with polio, and because polio is a child's illness, they kept every other kid away from me. I remember being pinned to this bed, and longing for friends and company."[3] Surely, this was a difficult way for a child to live. "When you had polio then, nobody brought their friends around; I was kept in a room by myself, and I used to read and occupy myself with puppets and mechanical things and gadgets; we had a tape recorder, a TV set, and things like that."[4]

Coppola contracted polio while on a Cub Scout trip and became paralyzed on his left side. While confined to his bed, he not only played with his puppets, but he also began making movies with his father's 8 mm movie camera. So, in a way his affliction with polio actually helped to shape his future.

7

Just When We Thought It Was Safe: Post-polio Syndrome

Thanks to the creation of the Salk and Sabin vaccines, the number of polio cases has consistently decreased since the 1950s. However, in the late 1970s, symptoms began to appear in people who had recovered from paralytic polio years earlier. The symptoms included pain in muscles and joints, excessive fatigue, and increased muscle weakness.

The doctors had never seen anything like this, except when these people originally contracted polio. They had no name for the condition and no way to treat it. It had always been believed that with rehabilitation and therapy most polio survivors would achieve a level of functioning that would remain the same for the rest of their lives. Now that belief was being turned upside down.

The number of cases of this strange **syndrome** kept increasing. When the data were studied, it was seen that the syndrome appeared 10 to 40 years after the patient had suffered from the **acute** illness. The doctors were stumped.

THE SYNDROME GETS A NAME

With the ever-increasing frequency of the syndrome, it was finally given a name. In the early 1980s, the term *post-polio syndrome* (PPS) was coined. It was defined as a neurological disorder with a variety of symptoms that occur in patients who recovered years earlier from a case of paralytic polio. The most serious symptom is a new case of progressive muscle weakness.

The actual cause of the symptoms is unknown. One theory is the death of individual motor nerve cells in the spinal cord that had survived the initial attack of polio. These cells had to take over the function of cells that were destroyed during the initial attack of the disease. In order to do this, they had to grow new branches so they could communicate with muscles that once received nerve impulses from the now-destroyed nerve cells. This extra work put a great strain on the remaining cells and they were highly susceptible to being destroyed (Figure 7.1).

Other possibilities include the reactivation of poliovirus in the central nervous system or an unregulated immune response to the prior infection. Motor nerve cells are responsible for transmitting the signal that comes down the spinal cord from the brain to nerves that go directly to muscles. The degree of severity of post-polio syndrome symptoms depends on how seriously the individual was affected by the actual case of polio in the first place and how many of these cells remained unaffected by the disease. Interestingly, it was found that PPS is brought about by serious stress to the body. This could be a fall, a disease that caused the patient to need extended bed rest, an accident, or surgery.

HOW IS IT DIAGNOSED?

Post-polio syndrome is difficult to diagnose accurately. Part of the problem is making sure that the muscle weakness is progressive. In order to determine this, the patient must make repeated visits to the doctor to document a continuous decrease in muscle strength.

Another problem that doctors face is trying to be objective about the progress of the muscle weakness. This can be very difficult, as there is no specific machine that can accurately

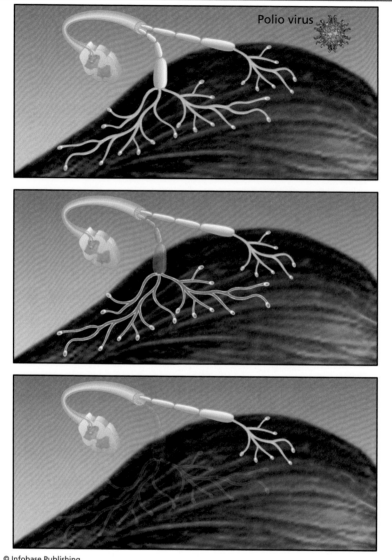

© Infobase Publishing

Figure 7.1   Post-polio syndrome causes progressive muscle weakness. When nerve cells die during the initial attack of polio, other nerve cells take over the job of the dead cells (top). In the middle panel, the branch on the left begins to degrade from the added strain of compensating for the cells killed in the intial polio attack. In the bottom panel, the branch on the left is completely dead.

determine if a muscle, or group of muscles, is getting weaker, or if the patient is just having a bad day. Doctors may use magnetic resonance imaging (MRI), neuroimaging, and electrophysiological studies to help make the diagnosis. In addition, a muscle **biopsy** may be performed. This test takes a sample of the tissue and looks at it under the microscope to see if the muscle is actually damaged.

The March of Dimes established specific criteria for the diagnosis of PPS.[1] Of course, the patient must have had prior paralytic polio with residual weakness and muscle atrophy demonstrated by a neuromuscular exam. In addition, signs of nerve damage should be noted when electromyography (EMG) is used as a diagnostic test. This test involves the use of needles placed into the muscle at different sites and the passage of an electric current through the muscle to determine its condition.

Another criterion set forth is a period of partial or complete recovery after a case of acute paralytic polio. This period should be followed by a time frame of at least 15 years of stable neuromuscular function.

If the patient suffers from a gradual onset of progressive and persistent new muscle weakness or decreased endurance, even if it is not accompanied by muscle atrophy or joint pain, then the doctor has one more indicator of PPS.

The symptoms associated with a positive diagnosis of PPS should last at least a year, and other neuromuscular orthopedic

DID YOU KNOW THAT . . .

In a study performed in 2002 at Haukeland University Hospital in Bergen, Norway, researchers found that some patients who had been diagnosed with non-paralytic polio between 1950 and 1954 are now showing motor weakness and symptoms similar to those seen in post-polio syndrome. The symptoms are similar to those associated with neuromuscular damage as is seen in PPS.[2]

or medical problems must be ruled out as causes of the symptoms.

Dr. Lauro Halstead, director of the post-polio syndrome program at the National Rehabilitation Hospital in Washington, D.C., describes the syndrome very clearly:

> My own experience seems to be typical of both recovery from paralytic polio and the new development of post-polio syndrome. I contracted polio during the epidemic of 1954 while traveling in Europe after my freshman year in college. I was 18 years old. My six-month journey of recovery took me from iron lung to wheelchair to foot brace and then to no assistive device at all. At times, improvement in strength seemed to happen overnight. Although my right arm remained paralyzed, the rest of my body regained most of the strength and endurance I had before my illness. As a result, I thought of myself as cured. I returned to college, learned to write with my left hand, and even played intramural squash. On the morning of the third anniversary of the onset of my polio, I reached the summit of Mount Fuji in Japan after a climb of over 12,000 feet. As I watched the sun rise, I thought, "Polio is behind me. I have finally conquered it."
>
> With the conquest of Mount Fuji fresh in my mind, I began to look for other mountains to climb. After college, I entered medical school. Internship and residency initiated yet another cycle of physically demanding years. In short, I got on with my life while polio receded ever further in my memory. Several years ago I began developing new weakness in my legs. As the weakness progressed over a period of months, I went from being a full-time walker who jogged up six flights of stairs for exercise to having to use a motorized scooter full-time at work.[3]

Although it took until the 1980s to give post-polio syndrome a name, the syndrome had previously been mentioned in a French medical journal. Unfortunately, when the syndrome appeared in large numbers in the twentieth century, nobody remembered the original reference. In fact, between 1875 and 1975 there were at least 35 references in as many medical journals.

In 1984, scientists held a conference at the Warm Springs Institute for Rehabilitation. This is the institute in Georgia that was started by Franklin Delano Roosevelt in 1926 to treat polio victims (Figure 7.2). He opened the clinic because he felt that swimming in warm water helped to strengthen weak muscles.

In 1986, another meeting was held that led to much more research into and understanding of post-polio syndrome. It stimulated interest in learning more about the syndrome as well. Even the United States government became involved. The National Center for Health Statistics, a group that collects data on diseases from households in the United States, calculated that there were more than 640,000 people who survived paralytic polio. This insight helped doctors to estimate the magnitude of the problem. Some research studies have claimed that as many as 40 percent of paralytic polio survivors may have post-polio syndrome. If this is true, there may be up to 250,000 people in the United States who are currently suffering from the syndrome.

With such a high number of people who probably suffer from the syndrome, the obvious question is, "Is there a treatment or a cure?" Although there are several treatment options for PPS, none of them brings about a true cure. Treatments may lessen or eliminate some of the problems associated with the syndrome.

Exercise is always good for the body and it is especially important for the patient with PPS. The exercise program must be non-fatiguing and designed to strengthen the muscles

Figure 7.2 In 1926, president Franklin Delano Roosevelt founded the Warm Springs Institute for Rehabilitation in Georgia because he believed the warm water and swimming would help polio victims. In the picture above, Roosevelt swims at the institute. Several polio symposia have also been held at this location. (© AP Images)

involved and improve their functioning. For some patients, gentle stretching or yoga prove to be effective. For others, mild aerobic training works. If a patient is too weak or fatigued from his or her normal daily routine, however, exercise should be avoided.

For cases of fatigue, a change in lifestyle is recommended. Adding rest periods and daytime naps can be very helpful. Discontinuing unnecessary activities, such as making the bed or washing the car, helps as well. In addition, overweight or obese people may find weight loss very beneficial. Also, if possible, a change in one's job or a reduction of hours may alleviate a good deal of the fatigue.

When pain accompanies a case of PPS, a number of different therapies are possible. If other conditions, such as arthritis or tendonitis, are responsible, they must be addressed with medication and a change in activities. If overuse of muscles is the cause, modifications in lifestyle or physical therapy may be called for. Ice packs, moist heat, and massage are often useful in alleviating much of the pain. In addition, pain medications have been prescribed with some success.

Any individual who has a breathing problem should avoid respiratory infections. In order to do this, annual flu shots and pneumonia vaccines are recommended. Equipment designed to aid in nighttime breathing may help the patient to sleep better and feel more energetic. Swallowing problems may be addressed by learning special techniques and by changing the diet in order to make swallowing easier.

WHO IS AT RISK?

Several factors help to determine the level of risk for developing post-polio syndrome. One of these is the severity of the initial infection. The more severe the infection, the greater the risk of developing the syndrome.

Another factor is the age of onset of the initial illness. It appears that people who were infected as children stand less of a chance of developing post-polio syndrome in their adult years. People who became infected as adolescents and adults have a much higher risk of developing PPS.

As strange as it may seem, the greater the recovery after an acute case of polio, the greater the chance of developing PPS. This may be directly related to lifestyle. A person who has recovered almost to the point where he or she was prior to the infection is more likely to attempt to live a normal life. This may put a greater strain on the motor neurons, causing them to break down more easily.

Finally, an individual who, on a regular basis, is physically active to the point of exhaustion will seriously challenge the already stressed-out motor neurons, thus increasing his or her risk of developing the syndrome.

WHAT ABOUT THE FUTURE?

Post-polio syndrome is known to progress slowly and is associated with periods of stability where no further progress occurs. In fact, eventually the patient experiences no change in status and no further paralysis occurs. Because of this clinical picture, PPS is usually not life threatening. Of course, there is also no return of the lost muscle function once it disappears.

One serious cause of concern occurs in those patients who have experienced damage to their respiratory muscles during a bout with polio. In these patients, any further weakening of respiratory muscles, as occurs in PPS, may cause serious breathing problems. If the degree of weakness is great, the patient may die of respiratory failure.

Although it is more common for patients who had bulbar palsy to develop swallowing problems, also called dysphagia, it has been discovered that some patients who had polio, but did not have any respiratory involvement, may still develop swallowing problems. There are several indicators for dysphagia, including loss of interest in eating, unintentional weight loss, difficulty swallowing tablets, coughing or choking when eating, and food sticking in the throat.[4]

Patients with dysphagia must be careful even after they eat; in some cases, residue may remain in the pharynx after eating and lead to choking later on. It may be necessary for the individual to change his or her position when eating in order to avoid collecting food in any area of the pharynx.

THE FAMOUS SUFFER HERE TOO
Joni Mitchell

As with polio, several famous people who had the disease now suffer from post-polio syndrome. One of these is

Joni Mitchell (Figure 7.3). She was born Roberta Joan Anderson on November 7, 1943, in Fort McLeod, Alberta, Canada. Mitchell is a well-known singer who has been performing for over 30 years. She was diagnosed with polio at the age of nine. Then, in the 1980s, she was diagnosed with post-polio syndrome.

When interviewed on September 9, 1998, Mitchell described how she is dealing with PPS:

> . . . the eighties were a rough decade for me and on top of it I was diagnosed as having post-polio syndrome, which they said was inevitable for I'm a polio survivor, that 40 years after you had the disease, which is a disease of the nervous system, the wires that animate certain muscles are taken out by the disease, and the body in its ingenious way, the filaments of the adjacent muscles send out branches and try to animate that muscle. It's kind of like the EverReady bunny, the muscles all around the muscles that are gone begin to go also because they've been trying to drive this muscle for so long. That's the nature of what was happening so I had it mostly in my back, so you don't see it as much as you would in a withered leg or an arm. But the weight of the guitar became unbearable. Also, acoustic guitar requires that you extend your shoulder out in an abnormal way and coincidentally some of the damage to my back in combination with that position was very painful. So, there was a merchant in Los Angeles who knew of my difficulties and knew that this machine was coming along that would solve my tuning problems and he made on spec a Stratocaster for me out of yellow cedar that was very light and thin as a wafer, so an electric guitar is a more comfortable design for my handicap. Then, a genius luthier built me this two and a half pound guitar which is not only beautiful to look at but it kind of contours to my body. It fits my hip and even kind of cups

Figure 7.3   Joni Mitchell suffers from post-polio syndrome. She has experienced muscle weakness in her back, which made it difficult to hold her guitar. She has coped with the pain and discomfort by having a guitar specially designed so it matches the contours of her body and places less stress on her back muscles. (© AP Images)

up like a bra! It's just beautifully designed and then also I abandoned regular medicine and fell into the hands first of a Kahuna and then a Chinese mystic acupuncturist who put down his pins and just points at you. I know this sounds real quacky but they did some mysterious good to the problem and I feel fine."[5]

It is encouraging to hear someone with post-polio syndrome explain how she is able to function well in spite of such a debilitating condition. Even with PPS, Mitchell has continued to perform and travel extensively.

Sir Arthur C. Clarke

Futurist, science fiction writer, and Renaissance man, Sir Arthur C. Clarke (Figure 7.4) was born in Minehead, Somerset, England, on December 16, 1917. He became a prolific writer of science fiction stories and articles relating to various topics in the field of science.

In 1956, Clarke settled in Sri Lanka. In 1959, he contracted polio, but that did not stop him from writing and lecturing. In 1968, one of his most famous novels, *2001: A Space Odyssey*, was made into a very successful movie. Toward the end of his life he suffered from post-polio syndrome and was confined to a wheelchair. Nevertheless, he was still very active in many areas including writing, observing the skies with a 14-inch telescope, playing table tennis, working with computers, and coming up with more futuristic ideas. His last novel, *Firstborn*, was published in 2007, when he was 90 years old. Clarke died in 2008.

HOW TO DEAL WITH THE PAIN

For the many people who are suffering from post-polio syndrome, pain is a constant companion. Post-Polio Health International has a list of recommendations to help patients cope with PPS:[6]

1. Moist heat applied to the painful area.

2. Light massage to the painful area.

3. Ice packs applied to the painful area.

Figure 7.4 Science fiction writer Arthur C. Clarke also suffered from post-polio syndrome 45 years after he initially contracted the disease. Toward the end of his life, he could no longer walk and used a wheelchair to get around. However, he continued to write and pursued an active lifestyle, including playing table tennis. (© AP Images)

4. Treatment of sleeping difficulties, i.e., insufficient amount of deep, Stage IV (REM) sleep.

5. Treatment of breathing difficulties, e.g., insufficient amount of oxygen and/or too much carbon dioxide, especially during sleep.

6. Use of assistive and adaptive aids, as necessary, to reduce stress and strain to muscles and joints; assuring that all body parts that require it—for example, neck, head, back, shoulders—are properly supported at all times.

7. Medications may also be used for muscle-joint inflammation and nerve pain (neuropathy).

Will these recommendations work for all patients? Unfortunately not, but by using one or more of these approaches to treatment, a good percentage of those who are suffering from post-polio syndrome will find some degree of relief.

8

What Lies Ahead? The Future of Polio

MAKING A VIRUS

If you needed to build a radio, you might go online and find a supplier or two that could provide you with the necessary parts. At some other Web site, you could probably even find the directions to do the work. It seems like a pretty simple concept. Who could ever imagine being able to go online and find the recipe to assemble a virus? Furthermore, who would think that the gene sequences needed would also be available from a mail-order supplier?

It may be mind boggling, but this is exactly what was announced on July 11, 2002, when Dr. Eckard Wimmer (Figure 8.1), a professor in the Department of Molecular Genetics at the State University of New York at Stony Brook, and his team announced that they had created an infectious virus in a test tube. The virus could successfully infect living cells. The virus was poliovirus.

Although much of the world's population today is concerned with bioterrorism, according to Dr. Wimmer the technique may be used for good purposes. He suggested that scientists might be able to create and prepare vaccines at a much faster rate than before and also perform gene therapy. In addition, biological attacks may be more easily avoided thanks to this new technique.

Dr. Wimmer is no stranger to the poliovirus. He has been conducting research on the virus for many years. He has also worked with other viruses, studying their methods for reproduction, which is referred to as

Figure 8.1 Using new DNA technologies, viruses can be created in the laboratory. Dr. Eckard Wimmer of the State University of New York at Stony Brook created a version of the poliovirus in a test tube. He believes that his extensive virus research will help scientists create better vaccines. (Courtesy Dr. Eckard Wimmer)

replication. Dr. Wimmer explained that he was able to purchase ready-made pieces of DNA from commercial sources. DNA is the genetic code that is found in all living creatures, from viruses right up to mankind itself (Figure 8.2). The letters stand for Deoxyribonucleic acid. It directs all processes of life,

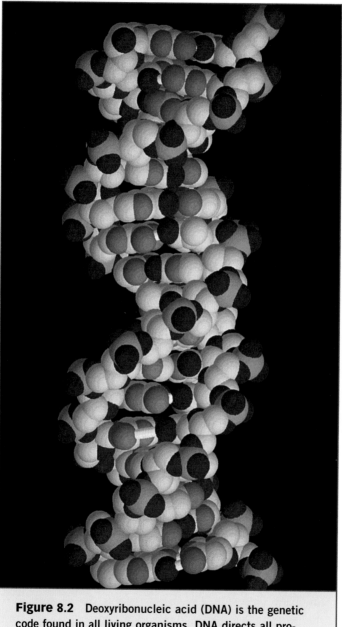

Figure 8.2   Deoxyribonucleic acid (DNA) is the genetic code found in all living organisms. DNA directs all processes of life, from what an organism looks like to how it functions. (© Tom Pantages/Visuals Unlimited)

including how a virus affects a living cell. A DNA *sequence* is the order of the base pairs that make up DNA. Four different chemicals, arranged in precisely the correct order in a variety of ways, make up our genes. Once a researcher knows the correct order for a particular virus, he or she may string the genes together and make the virus work. The DNA sequence information of many disease-causing organisms is available on the Web and may be used by any scientist who has the right knowledge, equipment, and money.

USING POLIOVIRUS FOR GOOD

In 1999, Dr. Matthias Gromeier and his research team used the poliovirus to help mankind. Surely, this was quite a dramatic departure from the virus's usual role as a disease-causing pathogen.

Dr. Gromeier knew that malignant glioma was the most common malignancy of the central nervous system. He was also aware of the fact that, in most cases, it resisted the available treatment options and had a very poor prognosis. Research in prior years had used viruses as delivery vehicles to allow genetic material to enter cells (gene therapy). Other research had shown that viruses could also be used as infectious agents that were toxic to tumor cells (viral oncolysis). As it turned out, poliovirus was one of these.

If poliovirus was to be used to destroy the malignant tumors, Dr. Gromeier and his team had to be sure that the introduction of the virus into the laboratory animals would not also damage the surrounding normal brain tissue. One of the problems that researchers face with this type of therapy is that viruses can only be grown in live tissue. Thus, the scientists can use either live tissue cultures or experimental animals with artificially developed tumor cells. That is, these animals do not normally grow these tumors on their own. Although researchers may have success with these animals, the results may not carry over to non-experimental animals that have developed gliomas naturally.

Viruses can only replicate by attaching themselves to specific protein receptor sites on the outside of cells. Different cells throughout the body have different receptor sites. Neural tissue has a receptor site known as CD155, which is an attachment point for poliovirus. Since gliomas are made from neural tissue, they also have these receptors. Poliovirus requires the CD155 receptor to attach to neural cells and infect them.

Dr. Gromeier's team manipulated the poliovirus in conjunction with the virus that causes the common cold (rhinovirus) so the experimental animals did not develop polio. Using the "body" of the polio virus as a means of attachment to the tumor cells, the manipulated virus was able to destroy the tumors. Of course, the body's own immune system, recognizing the presence of the virus, may also have helped in the tumor destruction.

Research on this fascinating and promising approach to tumor destruction is continuing in several laboratories throughout the world. In fact, the modified virus (known as PVS-RIPO) is used in investigational new drug-directed toxicology studies in preparation for Phase 1 clinical trials. "Phase 1 includes the initial introduction of an investigational new drug into humans. These studies are closely monitored and may be conducted in patients, but are usually conducted in healthy volunteer subjects. These studies are designed to determine the metabolic and pharmacologic actions of the drug in humans, the side effects associated with increasing doses, and, if possible, to gain early evidence on effectiveness. During Phase 1, sufficient information about the drug's pharmacokinetics and pharmacological effects should be obtained to permit the design of well-controlled, scientifically valid Phase 2 studies."[1]

YET ANOTHER LIFE-SAVING USE FOR POLIOVIRUS

In light of the fact that modern technology has enabled researchers to modify viruses, another team has been able to use attenuated poliovirus to destroy a different cancerous tumor. Neuroblastoma is the most common solid cancerous tumor occurring outside of the skull in childhood and the most common cancer in infancy. In fact, almost 50 percent of cases are found in children younger than two years of age. It accounts for approximately 15 percent of cancer deaths in children. Only 10 percent of the cases occur in people over the age of five.

Neuroblastomas may occur anywhere in the body, in places such as the abdomen, chest, spinal cord, and bones. The cause of this cancer is not known and many possibilities have been suggested and investigated, including parental occupational exposure to chemicals, as well as smoking, alcohol consumption, and use of certain medicines during pregnancy. None of the research has been conclusive, however.

Jeronimo Cello and Hidemi Toyoda, along with their team at the State University of New York at Stony Brook, used the attenuated poliovirus to attack neuroblastomas in mice. These cells, just like those of the malignant gliomas that Dr. Gromeier works with, contain the CD155 receptor site, thus allowing the virus to attach itself and introduce its genes into the tumor cells. When the cells began reproducing viruses they eventually died. In addition, the treatment apparently prevented the recurrence of the tumors and caused destruction of subsequently transplanted tumors.

The researchers were concerned about whether the virus would be able to destroy the neuroblastoma cells if the mice were previously vaccinated against polio. Their results showed that prior vaccination had no effect on the viruses' ability to infect the tumor cells. This is very encouraging as it indicates that, with further study, the procedure may be used in humans who have been vaccinated.

WORLDWIDE ERADICATION

As mentioned earlier, the occurrence of polio worldwide has diminished considerably thanks to the development of the Salk and Sabin vaccines. The World Health Organization had established a goal of worldwide polio **eradication** by the year 2000. Unfortunately, that year has come and gone, and polio still exists, although in small numbers.

India is one of the places where the disease is still prevalent. In 1995, the Indian government improved its vaccine program to include biannual National Immunization Days designed to vaccinate young children. This was done in an effort to meet the goals set by the WHO. More than 79 million children were vaccinated under this program in 1995 and another 134 million in 1998. However, in August 2002, polio cases in India tripled in the first half of the year compared with the same period one year earlier.

As of January 2008, India had actually failed to stop the spread of polio. The nation reported 676 cases in 2006 and 756 cases in 2007, an increase of 12 percent. There was, however, some positive news. India's most populous state, Uttar Pradesh, had initiated an aggressive vaccination program in 2006 to control the epidemic. Thanks to this effort, the state's health department reported 315 cases in 2007, down from 548 cases in 2006, a drop of 43 percent.

Unfortunately, the state of Bihar reported 396 cases of polio in 2007 after having seen only 61 cases in 2006. This was an increase of approximately 650 percent in one year. A Central Health Ministry official commented, "Uttar Pradesh has done really well in 2007, but the increase in the number of cases in Bihar is a worrying trend . . . However, we feel a weak immunization drive, lack of proper transportation facilities to many areas, and proximity to Uttar Pradesh are the main reasons behind the increased incidence in Bihar. It's certainly a major worry and we are going to focus on Bihar in 2008 without feeling complacent about Uttar Pradesh."[2]

In response to the increase in cases in Bihar, the World Health Organization and the Indian Health Ministry have devised a plan for Bihar. A concentration of efforts will be directed toward 72 high-prevalence blocks in eight districts.

"More surveillance, more manpower and a regular immunization drive will be carried out in Bihar. The first round [of the
year] was carried out in the second week of January [2008]. We
are going to carry out drives against both P1 and P3 strains,"
according to a World Health Organization official.

Polio also made its reappearance in another area of the
world. In October 2002, 27 children in the state of Kaduna,
Nigeria, developed new cases of polio. Kaduna had not
reported a single case of polio for the two previous years. In
fact, the nation reported 113 new cases of the 720 reported
worldwide by October. It is one of the countries worst hit by
polio. The outbreak prompted a renewed vaccination campaign
in an effort to stop any further spread of the disease.

Over the next several years, Nigeria continued to see new
cases of polio. Although the numbers decreased, the disease was
never completely eradicated. To completely stop the transmission of polio and eradicate it once and for all, the Nigerian government set May 2008 as its target date to finally wipe out the
disease. They set up a program called National Immunization
Plus Days (NIPDs), during which children would be vaccinated
against polio and receive other child survival interventions,
including distribution of insecticide-treated mosquito nets
(INTs), vitamin A, deworming tablets, and acetaminophen
syrup (used to reduce fevers and treat pain).

On January 26, 2008, Dr. Jide Idris, the Lagos, Nigeria, State
Commissioner for Health, addressed stakeholders at the kickoff of the first NIPD held at Ajeromi-Ifelodun. He stated that
"Between September and December 2007, Lagos State recorded
three outbreaks of WPV (Wild Polio Virus) in three local government areas (LGAs). Now, just a few days ago, another LGA
has been added to the list. This is not a cheering news at all
simply because the state had been declared polio free for over
24 months before the outbreaks."[3]

His explanation was that the small outbreak had been traced
to children missed during previous vaccination initiatives and

"zero dose" children, who had never received vaccinations. He urged parents to work toward avoiding this problem. "It is imperative to stress that Nigeria has set May 2008 to stop transmission of WPV in the whole country. Lagos is participating and shall be part of the success story. It is now behooved [sic] on every one of us to work together to ensure that every child is reached," he said.

At the January 26, 2008, kickoff of the NIPDs, the wife of the Lagos state governor, Abimbola Fashola, expressed her concern that despite all of the efforts to wipe out polio in Nigeria, many children are still dying of the disease. "It remains a matter of great concern that in spite of past efforts, our nation belongs to the group of very few countries in the world that has not been able to meet global targets of total polio eradication," she lamented. As of August 2008, there were 556 confirmed cases of polio in Nigeria, compared with 176 cases during the same period in 2007.[4] Unfortunately, this indicates that the initiative is not achieving its goals. More diligent efforts must be undertaken to stop the increase and spread of polio in Nigeria.

Polio has also reared its head in Pakistan, one of the four countries where polio has persisted. The Pakistani Health Ministry has been attempting to eradicate the disease without success. One of the problems that the government faces has occurred neither as a result of the disease nor as a result of patient noncompliance. Violence has plagued the country for many years, brought on by clashes between government forces and Taliban supporters, which has interfered with the Health Ministry's ability to immunize children.

In October 2007, the Health Ministry had a program established to immunize 350,000 children against polio in Pakistan's Swat Valley. The program had to be postponed until 2008 due to continuing violence in the area. The difficulty arose for two reasons. First, going to the area to administer vaccines put the teams at risk for injury or death. Secondly many of the inhabitants fled to safer areas of the country. In response, the government provided additional vaccines to districts where these children fled. During the week of October 29, 2007, the government had hoped to immunize 33.6 million children under five years of age nationwide, although that goal was not met.

The program was coordinated between the Pakistani government, the World Health Organization, and the United Nations International Children's Emergency Fund (UNICEF). In the first three days of the week, nearly 86,000 trained vaccination teams went door to door to administer oral polio vaccine. In addition, as in Nigeria, children between the ages of 6 months and 5 years also received vitamin A to enhance their immune systems.

Fortunately for the children, and the world in the long run, the program was launched on January 22, 2008. The World Health Organization has made it clear that eradicating polio worldwide is dependent on eliminating it from the four countries where it remains a threat: India, Pakistan, Nigeria, and Afghanistan.[5] Interviewed on the eve of the campaign, Ejaz Rahim, the Caretaker Federal Minister for Health said, "Active and visible commitment from political leaders, tribal leaders, religious leaders, the private sector, teachers, health workers, the media, and parents are [sic] important to reach every child."

Afghanistan is the fourth country where polio is still endemic (constantly present in a particular area). Luckily, the number of cases that occur annually is small compared to those seen in India, Pakistan, and Nigeria. However, an effective vaccination program is still of utmost importance if the disease is to be eradicated from this nation.

There are several roadblocks faced by health care workers when they attempt to vaccinate the population. Perhaps the most extensive is the presence of the Taliban. They have continued to block passage into many areas so effective vaccination cannot take place. Also, due to the war, many people continue to flee their homes and migrate to other areas. This creates the threat of virus exchange through the mobile populations.

Another difficulty in maintaining a successful vaccination program is an increase in refusals by parents. Although health care workers attempt to explain the benefits of the vaccine and clearly point out the risks associated with not getting vaccinated, a large number of the inhabitants remain unconvinced and will not get vaccinated or allow their children to be vaccinated.[6]

It should be noted that although India, Pakistan, Afghanistan, and Nigeria are the four nations where polio is still endemic, other countries continue to report sporadic cases

Table 8.1   World Polio Cases 2007–2008

Country	Year to date 2008	Year to date 2007	Total in 2007	Date of onset of most recent case
Afghanistan	3	0	17	February 9, 2008
India	106	11	866	February 7, 2008
Nigeria	28	14	286	January 26, 2008
Pakistan	2	5	32	January 25, 2008
Niger	3	1	11	January 23, 2008
Nepal	2	0	5	January 17, 2008
Angola	1	0	8	January 10, 2008
Chad	1	0	21	January 3, 2008
DRC	0	2	41	November 20, 2007
Sudan	0	0	1	September 10, 2007
Myanmar	0	0	11	May 28, 2007
Somalia	0	2	8	March 25, 2007

throughout the year. Table 8.1 lists all countries where polio was identified in 2007 and early 2008.[7]

HOW WILL THE FUTURE OF POLIO CHANGE?

Now the question is just how will the reappearance of polio affect the future of the polio eradication project? Certainly, the increase in the number of new cases, small as it is, means that the eradication program is not moving along as fast as world health leaders and the WHO had hoped. Further improvements in the surveillance of the vaccination program will help to slow down and eventually stop the new cases from occurring.

Thanks to an amazing amount of cooperation between government officials, the World Health Organization, financial institutions, and the public, polio is close to global eradication. However, scientists have made several predictions concerning the future of this goal.

As already mentioned, Sabin's oral polio vaccine is made with attenuated virus. This means that the virus, although weakened, is still alive. This allows for the possibility of reversion back to the active or **virulent** form of the virus that can infect people. This reversion may come about through mutation (a spontaneous change in the virus's DNA) or by recombination with other forms of the virus that would provide the necessary genetic information to become active once again.

If this reversion occurs in a person who has been vaccinated, he or she may spread the virus through feces and never know. After all, the person was vaccinated and developed antibodies, so he or she would not develop any symptoms. In such a case, this person would be referred to as a *healthy carrier*.

As mentioned earlier, the possibility of reactivation of attenuated virus is the reason for the exclusive use of inactivated polio vaccine (Salk) in the United States. Unfortunately, the countries where polio is **endemic** are still using oral polio vaccine in large quantities for their eradication programs. The ease of storage and delivery make the use of this type of vaccine a logical choice.

ROADBLOCKS AHEAD

In addition to the difficulties faced by the Eradication Initiative already mentioned, there remains a major, very basic roadblock to the successful eradication of polio from all countries. That difficulty is lack of money.

Between November 2007 and January 2008, the Global Polio Eradication Initiative received new contributions totaling nearly $190 million.[8] This funding will allow the initiative to achieve the following goals:

- Curbing transmission of type 1 poliovirus globally (widely regarded as the more dangerous of the two remaining serotypes, due to its higher paralytic attack rate and propensity for geographic spread), with an 84 percent decrease over the previous year—2007 is the year with the lowest-ever recorded incidence of type 1 polio;

- Reducing type 1 transmission in some of the most historically important type 1 reservoirs (such as western Uttar Pradesh, India, where no type 1 has been reported in over a year; and northern Nigeria, which saw a 90 percent reduction in type 1 polio over the previous year);

- Restricting polio transmission in the four remaining endemic countries (Nigeria, India, Pakistan, and Afghanistan) to specific, geographically limited areas; and,

- Stopping outbreaks in previously polio-free areas (of 27 re-infected countries since 2003, only six continued to report cases in the latter half of 2007: Angola, Chad, DR Congo, Nepal, Niger, and Sudan).

The contributions to the Global Polio Eradication Initiative in late 2007 and early 2008 are only the beginning. More assistance is needed to ensure the continued progress toward the eradication of polio. Although it is hoped that the disease will be eliminated by the end of 2008, a plan has to be in place that will cover several years of a continued initiative.

The table below helps one to understand the incredible financial challenges ahead for the success of the program through 2012.

Table 8.2 **Summary of External Financial Resource Requirements by Major Category of Activity, 2008–2012**

Activity Category	2008	2009	2008–2009	2010–2012
Oral polio vaccine	248.74	182.34	431.07	–
NIDs/SNIDs operations*	232.70	171.64	404.34	–
Emergency response/ mOPV evaluation	45.00	45.00	90.00	95.00
Surveillance	60.56	57.89	118.45	138.87
Laboratory	8.18	8.26	16.44	20.61
Technical assistance**	93.40	81.79	175.19	191.78
Certification and containment	–	5.00	5.00	30.00
Product development for OPV cessation	8.45	8.45	16.90	15.00
Vaccine for post-eradication era stockpile (product development and bulk)	–	49.22	49.22	–
Subtotal	**697.02**	**609.59**	**1306.61**	**491.26**
Contributions	525.06	255.74	780.80	–
Funding gap	**171.96**	**353.85**	**525.81**	**491.26**
Funding gap (rounded)	**175.00**	**350.00**	**525.00**	**490.00**

(figures are in US$ millions)

* Operations costs include manpower and incentives, training and meetings, supplies and equipment, transportation, social mobilization and running costs.

** Technical assistance includes the cost of human resources deployed through UN agencies.

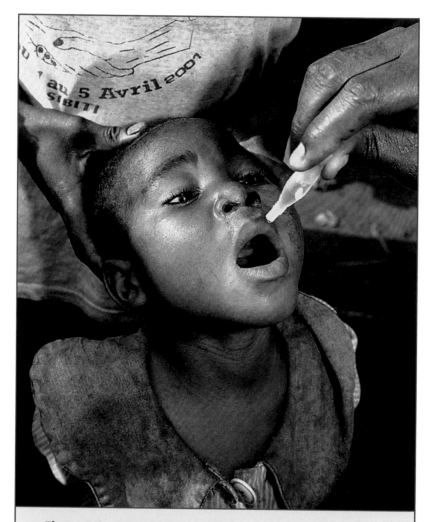

Figure 8.3 Although polio has been eradicated in the United States, it is still endemic in India, Pakistan, Afghanistan, and Nigeria. In addition, imported cases exist in several other nations in sub-Saharan Africa. The World Health Organization and the Global Polio Eradication Initiative are attempting to fully eradicate type 1 polio by the end of 2008 and type 2 polio by the end of 2009. The mass immunization program will use oral polio vaccine (OPV). The young African boy shown here is receiving OPV, which has dramatically decreased the number of polio cases in Africa. (Courtesy WHO/Sven Torfinn)

WHEN WILL IT ALL END?

In order for polio to be considered totally eradicated from the face of the Earth, the Global Polio Eradication Initiative has established specific requirements. The first step is containment of the virus, which has four parts: [9]

1. National authorities in all countries survey laboratories to identify those with wild poliovirus infectious or potentially infectious materials and encourage destruction of all unneeded materials.

2. Laboratories retaining such materials institute enhanced biosafety level-2 procedures. This means that laboratory personnel have specific training in handling pathogenic agents and are directed by competent scientists; access to the laboratory is limited when work is being conducted; extreme precautions are taken with contaminated sharp items; and certain procedures in which infectious aerosols or splashes may be created are conducted in biological safety cabinets or other physical containment equipment.

3. National authorities develop a national inventory of all laboratories with wild poliovirus materials.

4. Member states begin planning for implementation of biosafety requirements for the post-eradication phase.

The second step is certification. This is the independent verification of wild poliovirus eradication. The WHO established a Global Certification Commission in 1995. This commission studies all aspects of the eradication program and determines whether or not polio has, indeed, been eradicated from the Earth. This will happen when three years have elapsed with zero new cases of wild poliovirus infection.

The third step is to establish a post-eradication immunization policy. This policy will be determined by the WHO member states. Information will include the amount of vaccine on hand

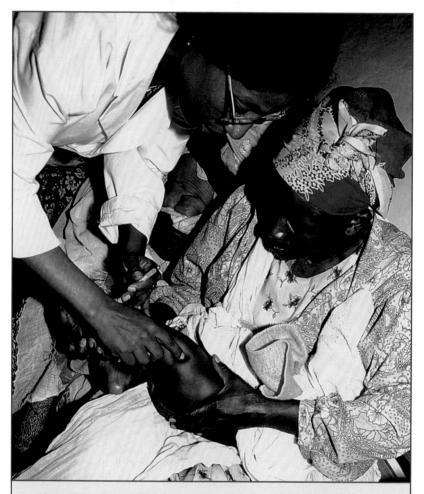

Figure 8.4 The Global Polio Eradication Initiative has established four steps toward the eradication of polio: immunization with the oral vaccine, booster vaccines to ensure continued immunity, "mop-up campaigns" to prevent transmission of the virus from those who already have it to those who may not have full immunity, and continued surveillance of areas where polio may still be present in some form (for example, polioviruses in the water supply or non-symptomatic carriers). Since 50 percent of polio cases affect children under the age of three, it is especially important that this group receives immunizations, such as the young Ethiopian boy shown here. (Courtesy WHO/P. Virot)

throughout the world, production capacity, and potential costs of making more vaccine.

One last consideration relating to the future of polio is that of terrorism. In light of the many recent occurrences of terrorist acts throughout the world and the specific question of bioterrorism, many have asked whether or not polio might be one of the viruses that terrorists could use to threaten the world.

Scientists agree that the largest viral threat is that of smallpox, a disease that has been eradicated from the Earth thanks to an extensive vaccination program worldwide. They believe that polio, although a possible threat, is very low on the list of viruses to be concerned about due to its low overall rate of causing disease in the people it infects.

Nevertheless, the question of polio's role in bioterrorism has contributed to the debate over whether or not, once polio is officially eradicated globally, the vaccine should still be administered worldwide.

In light of the fact that many countries are still administering oral polio vaccine (OPV), which in some cases has been shown to acquire the transmission characteristics of wild poliovirus, stopping vaccination would leave unvaccinated individuals at risk of developing the full-blown disease from viruses shed by vaccinated people. Cases such as these are termed vaccine-derived polioviruses (VDPVs). This is an excellent argument for continuing to vaccinate the public after naturally occurring polio has been officially eradicated from the world.

In many countries, as mentioned previously, only inactivated poliovirus vaccine (IPV) is being administered due to the risks associated with OPV. This will not eliminate the threat associated with long-term carriers of the live virus—acquired either from OPV or a prior natural infection—that they may cause infection in non-vaccinated individuals. This mode of infection is referred to as circulating vaccine-derived poliovirus (cVDPV). Although rare, these carriers do exist in the population and still pose a threat that cannot be ignored.

One study in the United Kingdom described two people with immune disorders who shed live virus for 32 and 21 months, respectively.[10] As a result of that study, a registry was established by WHO to keep records on individuals who shed virus for extended periods of time. Those included in the registry have shown shedding of virus for periods ranging from six months to ten years. Surely, this is reason enough to continue the vaccination program long after polio is considered to have been eradicated. The WHO will develop guidelines for considering when it might be safe to stop vaccinating.

Notes

Chapter 1

1. J. G. Lockheart, *Memoirs of Sir Walter Scott* (Edinburgh: A. and C. Black, 1882).
2. M. A. Underwood, *Treatise on the Diseases of Children with General Directions for the Management of Infants from Birth*, 2nd ed. (London: Mathews, 1789).
3. S. Flexner and P. A. Lewis, "The Transmission of acute poliomyelitis to monkeys," *Journal of the American Medical Association* 53 (1909): 1639.

Chapter 2

1. Elizabeth Kenny, *And They Shall Walk: The Life Story of Sister Elizabeth Kenny* (New York: Dodd, 1943).

Chapter 4

1. Interview with Jonas Salk, May 16, 1991, http://www.achievement.org/autodoc/page/sal0bio-1 (accessed March 3, 2008).
2. Bonnie A. Maybury Okonek and Linda Morganstein, "Development of Polio Vaccines," *The National Health Museum* (2002), http://www.accessexcellence.org/AE/AEC/CC/polio.html (accessed March 3, 2008).

Chapter 5

1. Ronald Reagan, presentation ceremony for the Presidential Medal of Freedom, May 12, 1986, http://www.reagan.utexas.edu/archives/speeches/1986/51286b.htm (accessed March 3, 2008).

Chapter 6

1. Bridget Byrne, "Alan Alda Smoothly Shifts Gears," *SouthCoast Today*, http://archive.southcoasttoday.com/daily/04-01/04-08-01/e06li150.htm (accessed August 7, 2008).
2. Jack Riemer, "Playing Violin with Three Strings," *Houston Chronicle*, February 10, 2001.
3. Gene D. Phillips, *Godfather: The Intimate Francis Ford Coppola* (Lexington, Ky.: University Press of Kentucky, 2004).
4. Robert Lindsey, "Francis Ford Coppola: Promises to Keep," *New York Times Magazine*, July 24, 1988.

Chapter 7

1. Post-Polio Health International, "Post-polio Syndrome: Identifying Best Practices in Diagnosis and Care," June 4, 2001, http://www.post-polio.org/edu/modreps.html (accessed July 1, 2008).
2. T. Rekland et al., "Long-term follow-up of patients with nonparalytic poliomyelitis," *Archives of Physical Medicine and Rehabilitation* 83, 4 (April 2002): 533–537.
3. Lauro Halstead (ed.), *Managing Post-polio: A Guide to Living Well with Post-polio Syndrome* (Falls Church, Va.: NRH Press and ABI Professional Publications, 1998).
4. John Latham et al., *Post Polio Syndrome Management and Treatment in Primary Care* (Dublin, Ireland: Post Polio Support Group, 2007).
5. Interview with Joni Mitchell on KGSR-FM, Los Angeles, Calif., September 8, 1998, http://jonimitchell.com/library/view.cfm?id=1362 (accessed February 18, 2008).
6. Frederick Maynard and Joan Headley (eds.), "Handbook on the Late Effects of Poliomyelitis for Physicians and Survivors," *Post-polio Health International* (1999), http://www.post-polio.org/edu/handbk/alter.html (accessed on February 18, 2008).

Chapter 8

1. Center for Drug Evaluation and Research, "The CDER Handbook," United States Food and Drug Administration, http://www.fda.gov/cder/handbook/ (accessed February 21, 2008).
2. Prashant K. Nanda, "Polio Persists: Bihar Surpasses Uttar Pradesh," *India eNews*, January 27, 2008, http://www.indiae-news.com/health/20080127/94089.htm (accessed February 28, 2008).
3. Chioma Obinna and Lilian Elaye, "Nigeria: LSG Committed to May 2008 Polio Target," *Vanguard*, January 29, 2008, http://allafrica.com/stories/200801290432.html (accessed March 6, 2008).

Notes

4. Centers for Diesase Control and Prevention, "Progress Toward Poliomyelitis Eradication—Nigeria, January 2007–August 12, 2008," *Morbidity and Mortality Weekly Report*, August 29, 2008, http://www.cdc.gov/mmwk/preview/mmwrhtml/mm5734a4.htm (accessed September 21, 2008).

5. Reuters, "Pakistan: Over 30 Million Children to Be Vaccinated against Polio," *IRIN* (UN Office for the Coordination of Humanitarian Affairs), January 22, 2008.

6. Chris Morry, "Technical Consultation on Polio Eradication in Afghanistan and Pakistan," *The Communication Initiative Network*, October 1–2, 2007, http://www.comminit.com/en/node/265874 (accessed March 7, 2008).

7. Global Polio Eradication Initiative, "Wild Poliovirus Weekly Update," March 4, 2008, http://www.polioeradication.org/casecount.asp (accessed March 7, 2008).

8. Global Polio Eradication Initiative, *"Financial Resource Requirements for 2008–2012,"* January 15, 2008, http://www.polioeradication.org/fundingbackground.asp (accessed March 8, 2008).

9. World Health Organization, *WHO Global Action Plan for Laboratory Containment of Wild Poliovirus*, 2nd ed. (Geneva: World Health Organization, January 2004), http://www.polioeradication.org/content/publications/WHO-VB-03-729.pdf (accessed March 12, 2008).

10. R. W. Sutter, V. M. Cáceres, and P. Mas Lago, "The Role of Routine Polio Immunization in the Post-certification Era," *Bulletin of the World Health Organization* 82, 1 (January, 2004), http://www.who.int/bulletin/volumes/82/1/31-39.pdf (accessed March 13, 2008).

acute—Having a rapid onset and following a short but severe course.

antibody—A protein on the surface of B cells (one form of white blood cells) that is secreted into the blood or lymph in response to an antigenic stimulus, such as a bacterium, virus, parasite, or transplanted organ, and that neutralizes the antigen by binding specifically to it.

anamnestic—A secondary response of the immune system, it occurs when the immune system recognizes an antigen to which it has already formed antibodies.

antigen—A substance that, when introduced into the body, stimulates the production of an antibody. Antigens include toxins, bacteria, foreign blood cells, and the cells of transplanted organs.

aseptic—Free of pathogenic microorganisms. Usually refers to the absence of bacteria as opposed to the absence of viruses.

aseptic meningitis—Another name for nonparalytic polio.

asymptomatic—Not showing any symptoms of a disease.

attenuate—To weaken.

biopsy—The removal and examination of a sample of tissue from a living body for diagnostic purposes.

bioterrorism—The use of biological agents, such as pathogenic organisms or agricultural pests, for terrorist purposes.

carrier—A person or an animal that shows no symptoms of a disease but harbors the infectious agent of that disease and is capable of transmitting it to others.

disease—A pathological condition of a part, organ, or system of an organism resulting from various causes, such as infection, genetic defect, or environmental stress, and characterized by an identifiable group of signs or symptoms.

endemic—Naturally prevalent in a specific area.

epidemic—When a disease spreads rapidly and extensively by infection and affects many individuals in an area or a population at the same time.

eradication—The complete destruction or removal of something.

formaldehyde—A colorless compound used in embalming fluids and as a preservative and disinfectant.

Glossary

immobilization—To fix the position of a joint or limb, as with a splint or cast, so it cannot be moved.

infection—Invasion of the body by pathogenic organisms followed by their multiplication.

inflammation—A localized, protective reaction of tissue to irritation, injury, or infection. Characterized by pain, redness, swelling, and sometimes loss of function.

influenza—An acute contagious viral infection characterized by inflammation of the respiratory tract and by fever, chills, muscular pain, and prostration.

leukocyte—A white blood cell; part of the body's immune system; there are several types of leukocytes.

lymphocyte—Part of the immune system; one of the several types of white blood cells produced by humans that act to remove foreign organisms from the body; divided into B and T lymphocytes that are both essential to proper immune function.

macrophage—One of the several types of white blood cells in humans; a large cell that seeks out and engulfs foreign particles and cells through phagocytosis; part of the human body's immune system.

medulla oblongata—A portion of the brain stem; controls breathing and other vital functions, such as circulation of the blood.

microbiology—The branch of biology that deals with microorganisms and their effects on other living organisms.

microorganism—An organism of microscopic or submicroscopic size, especially a bacterium, virus, or protozoan.

mode of transmission—The mechanism by which a disease is passed from one person to another.

neutrophil—Part of the body's immune system; a type of white blood cell that rids the body of foreign invaders through the process of phagocytosis.

paralysis—Loss or impairment of the ability to move a body part, usually as a result of damage to its nerve supply.

phagocytosis—The process by which a white blood cell engulfs and literally "eats" a foreign body.

replicate—To reproduce or make an exact copy or copies.

sign—Observable indicator of a disease.

spasm—A sudden, involuntary contraction of a muscle or group of muscles.

subunit vaccine—A type of vaccine created by isolating specific antigens or parts of antigens of the foreign substance and introducing these into the body to form antibodies.

symptom—A sign or an indication of disorder or disease, especially when experienced by an individual as a change from normal function, sensation, or appearance.

syndrome—A group of symptoms that collectively indicate or characterize a disease, psychological disorder, or other abnormal condition.

tetanus—A type of bacterial disease that causes muscle spasms and paralysis.

toxoid—A substance that has been treated to destroy its toxic properties but retains the capacity to stimulate production of antitoxins, used in immunization.

vaccine—A substance used as a preventive inoculation to stimulate immunity against a specific disease.

virulent—Capable of causing disease.

Bibliography

Books and Articles

Associated Press. "Setback in the War on Polio." *Newsday* (August 13, 2002): A16.

Cooke, Robert. "A Virus Made from Scratch." *Newsday* (July 12, 2002): A8, A49.

Halstead, Lauro. *Managing Post-polio Syndrome: A Guide to Living Well with Post-polio Syndrome*. Arlington, Va.: ABI Professional Publishers, 1998.

Paul, John. *A History of Poliomyelitis*. New Haven, Conn.: Yale University Press, 1971.

Sass, Edmund. *Polio's Legacy: An Oral History*. Lanham, Md.: University of America Press, 1996.

Web Sites

Albert Sabin Biography
http://www.jewishvirtuallibrary.org/jsource/biography/Sabin.html

Eckard Wimmer
http://www.abc.net.au/am/stories/5605113.htm

Edward Jenner Biography
http://www.sc.edu/library/spcoll/nathist/jenner1.html

Epidemiology of Polio
http://cumicro2.cpmc.columbia.edu/PICO/Chapters/Epidemiology.html

Famous People with Polio
http://www.geocities.com/arojann.geo/poliopeople.html

FDR's Disability
http://webweekly.hms.harvard.edu/archive/2000/9_25/upcoming.html

History of FDR's Polio
http://www.feri.org/archives/polio/default.cfm

How Viruses Work
http://www.howstuffworks.com/virus-human.htm

Jonas Salk Biography
http://www.achievement.org/autodoc/page/sal0bio-1

Jonas Salk Biography
http://www.notablebiographies.com/Ro-Sc/Salk-Jonas.html

Making Vaccines
http://www.pbs.org/wgbh/nova/bioterror/vaccines.html

Polio
http://www.brown.edu/Courses/Bio_160/Projects1999/polio/main.html

Polio History Timeline
http://www.cloudnet.com/~edrbsass/poliotimeline.htm

Polio in Afghanistan
http://www.afghan-web.com/articles/poliomy.html

Post-polio Syndrome
http://www.ott.zynet.co.uk/polio/lincolnshire/library/halstead/sciampps.html

Quote from Presidential Medal of Freedom Ceremony
http://www.reagan.utexas.edu/archives/speeches/1986/51286b.htm

Sabin Vaccine Institute
http://www.sabin.org

Salk Produces Polio Vaccine
http://www.pbs.org/wgbh/aso/databank/entries/dm52sa.html

Sister Kenny: Polio Pioneer
http://www.ott.zynet.co.uk/polio/lincolnshire/library/drhenry/srkenny.html

University of Leicester, Department of Microbiology
http://www-micro.msb.le.ac.uk

Wilma Rudolph Biography
http://www.lkwdpl.org/wihohio/rudo-wil.htm

Further Resources

Books and Articles

Backman, Margaret E. *The Post-polio Experience: Psychological Insights and Coping Strategies for Polio Survivors and Their Families.* Lincoln, Nebr.: iUniverse, Inc., 2006.

Bredeson, Carmen. *Jonas Salk: Discoverer of the Polio Vaccine.* Hillside, N.J.: Enslow Press, 1993.

Brookes, Tim, and Omar A. Khan. *The End of Polio? Behind the Scenes of the Campaign to Vaccinate Every Child On the Planet.* Washington, D.C.: American Public Health Association Press, 2006.

Bruno, Richard L. *The Polio Paradox: Understanding and Treating "Post-polio Syndrome" and Chronic Fatigue.* New York: Time Warner Book Group, 2003.

Burge, Michael, and Don Nardo. *Vaccines: Preventing Disease.* San Diego, Calif.: Lucent Books, 1992.

Cowie, Peter. *Coppola.* New York: Scribner, 1990.

Dolan, Edward. *Jenner and the Miracle of Vaccine.* New York: Dodd, Mead, 1960.

Farrow, Mia. *What Falls Away: A Memoir.* New York: Nan A. Tavese, 1997.

Finger, Anne. *Elegy for a Disease: A Personal and Cultural History of Polio.* New York: St. Martin's Press, 2006.

Gould, Jean. *A Good Fight: The Story of F.D.R.'s Conquest of Polio.* New York: Dodd, Mead, 1960.

Halstead, Lauro S. *Managing Post-polio: A Guide to Living and Aging Well with Post-polio Syndrome.* Washington, D.C.: National Rehabilitation Hospital Press, 2006.

Huff, Carol. *Adelia: Simple Person, Silent Teacher, Polio Survivor.* Lincoln, Nebr.: iUniverse, Inc., 2007.

Kehret, Peg. *Small Steps: The Year I Got Polio.* Morton Grove, Ill.: Albert Whitman, 2006.

Kenny, Elizabeth. *And They Shall Walk: The Life Story of Sister Elizabeth Kenny.* New York: Dodd, 1943.

Kluger, Jeffrey. *Splendid Solution: Jonas Salk and the Conquest of Polio.* New York: Penguin Group, 2005.

Marx, Joseph. *Keep Trying: A Practical Book for the Handicapped.* New York: Hagan and Rowe, 1974.

Maus, Richard. *Lucky One: Making It Past Polio and Despair.* Northfield, Minn.: Anterior, 2006.

McDonough, Jimmy. *Shakey: Neil Young's Biography.* New York: Villard Books, 2002.

Nichols, Janice Flood. *Twin Voices: A Memoir of Polio, the Forgotten Killer.* Lincoln, Nebr.: iUniverse, 2007.

Offitt, Paul A. *The Cutter Incident: How America's First Polio Vaccine Led to the Growing Vaccine Crisis.* Chicago: R.R. Donnelly and Sons, 2005.

Oshinsky, David M. *Polio: An American Story.* New York: Oxford University Press, 2005.

Rains, A. J. Harding. *Edward Jenner and Vaccination.* London: Priory Press, 1974.

Rosenberg, Nancy, and Louis Cooper. *Vaccines and Viruses.* New York: Grosset and Dunlap, 1971.

Seavy, Nina G., Jane Smith, and Paul Wagner. *A Paralyzing Fear: The Triumph over Polio in America.* New York: TV Books, 1998.

Shell, Marc. *Polio and Its Aftermath: The Paralysis of Culture.* Cambridge, Mass.: Harvard University Press, 2005.

Silver, Julie, and Daniel J. Wilson. *Polio Voices: An Oral History from the American Polio Epidemics and Worldwide Eradication Efforts (The Praeger Series on Contemporary Health and Living).* Westport, Conn.: Greenwood, 2007.

Strait, Raymond. *Alan Alda: A Biography.* New York: St. Martin's Press, 1983.

Thomlinson, Michael. *Jonas Salk.* Vero Beach, Fla.: Rourke, 1993.

Weaver, Lydia. *Close to Home: A Story of the Polio Epidemic.* New York: Viking Press, 1993.

Wilson, Daniel J. *Living with Polio: The Epidemic and Its Survivors.* Chicago: University of Chicago Press, 2005.

Web Sites

Albert Sabin
http://www.cincinnnatichildrens.org/About/History/sabin.htm

Centers for Disease Control and Prevention
http://www.cdc.gov/polio

Further Resources

Development of Polio Vaccines
http://www.accessexcellence.org/AE/AEC/CC/polio.html

Edward Jenner and Vaccination
http://www.sc.edu/library/spcoll/nathist/jenner.html

Franklin Delano Roosevelt and Polio
http://www.hhmi.org/biointeractive/disease/polio/polio2.html

Global Polio Eradication
http://www.polioeradication.org

Jonas Salk
http://www.achievement.org/autodoc/page/sal0bio-1

Polio Experience Network
http://www.polionet.org

Post-polio Syndrome Central
http://www.skally.net/ppsc

Wild Poliovirus Weekly Update
http://www.polioeradication.org/casecount.asp

World Health Organization
http://www.who.int/en

Index

leg braces, 60, 61
leukocyte, 32. *See also* neutrophil
Leventritt Competition, 62
Lewis, Paul, 16
LGAs (local government areas), 89
life span, U.S. average, 31
Lister Institute (London, England), 49
live attenuated polio vaccine. *See* oral polio vaccine (OPV)
live tissue cultures, 85
local government areas (LGAs), 89
Lovett, Robert W., 22, 29
Luke, Book of, 10
lungs, 27
lymphocyte, 32, 33, 35

macrophage, 32–33
magnetic resonance imaging (MRI), 71
malignant glioma, 85–86
Man Unfolding (Salk), 47–48
March of Dimes, 46, 71
massage, for PPS, 75, 79
Matthew, Book of, 10–11
medulla oblongata, 25–27
Meharry Hospital (Tennessee), 61
meningitis, 40
meningococcal meningitis A, 41
Metropolitan Opera (New York City), 65
mice, 87
microbiologist, 42
microorganism, 31, 32, 39
Middle East, 36
milkmaids, 37
Mitchell, Joni, 76–79
mode of entry, 50
mode of transmission, 16, 18
moist heat, for PPS, 75, 79

monkeys, 16
Montagu, Mary Wortley, 36
motor neurons, 69, 76
motor weakness. *See* muscle weakness
movie director, 66–67
MRI (magnetic resonance imaging), 71
mucosal immunity, 51
muscle atrophy, 71
muscle biopsy, 71
muscles, paralysis of, 26
muscle weakness, 69–71
musicians, 61–65, 76–79

nasal passages, 16, 50
National Center for Health Statistics, 73
National Foundation for Infantile Paralysis (NFIP), 30, 44
National Immunization Days (India), 88
National Immunization Plus Days (Nigeria), 89, 90
National Institutes of Health, 54
National Medal of Science, 54
National Science Foundation, 46
Nelmes, Sara, 37
nerve cells, 70
nerve pain, 81
neural tissue, 86
neuroblastoma, 86–87
neuroimaging, 71
neuromuscular exam, 71
neuropathy, 81
neutrophil, 32, 33
New York University College of Dentistry, 49
New York University School of Medicine, 42, 49
NFIP. *See* National Foundation for Infantile Paralysis (NFIP)

Nigeria, 89–91
Nixon, Richard, 54
nonparalytic polio, 24, 50–51, 71
nose. *See* nasal passages

Olympic Games (1956), 61
Olympic Games (Rome, 1960), 60, 61
oncolysis, viral, 85
oral polio vaccine (OPV) (live attenuated polio vaccine; Sabin vaccine), 96
  creation/production of, 39–40
  disadvantages of, 51–52
  field tests, 51, 54
  lack of U.S. acceptance of, 51
  lives saved by, 55
  mutation potential of attenuated virus, 93
  polio eradication in U.S., 30
  Salk vaccine v., 51–54, 93
  use in developing countries, 93
  and VAPP, 51–52
orthopox virus family, 37

pain, PPS and, 75, 79, 81
Pakistan, 90–91
Pakistani Health Ministry, 90–91
paralysis, 10, 19, 26
paralytic polio
  effect on human body, 24–27
  and post-polio syndrome diagnosis, 71
  symptoms, 18–19, 24, 26
  Type 1 polio, 50
Paterson, New Jersey, 49
Perlman, Itzhak, 61–65
pertussis, 40
phagocytes, 32–34
phagocytosis, 32–34

Index

Phase 1 clinical trials, 86
Phipps, James, 37, 39
physical therapy, 27
picornavirus, 50
placebo, 45–46
plasma cell, 35
pneumococcal disease, 41
pneumonia, 40
pneumonia vaccination, 75
polio cases, worldwide
    (2007–2008), 92
poliovirus
    attenuated, 40
    and CD155 receptor site,
        86
    discovery of, 14–16
    effect on human body,
        24–27
    electron micrograph of, 23
    and immunocompro-
        mised patients, 100
    laboratory synthesis of,
        82–83, 85
    Landsteiner and Popper's
        hypothesis, 14–16
    post-polio syndrome, 69
    Albert Sabin's study of,
        49
    in small intestine, 18
    for treating cancer and
        other diseases, 85–87
polysaccharides, 41
Popper, Ervin, 14–16
Post-Polio Health
    International, 79, 81
post-polio syndrome (PPS),
    68–81
    diagnosis, 69, 71–72
    Joni Mitchell and, 76–79
    risk factors, 75–76
    treatment for, 73–75
Presidential Medal of
    Freedom, 54, 56
primary response, 35
progressive muscle weak-
    ness, 69–71
protein, 24, 41
protein coat, 23–24, 35

protein receptor site. *See*
    receptor site
pustules, 36, 38, 39
PVS-RIPO, 86

rabies vaccine, 49
Rahim, Ejaz, 91
Reagan, Ronald, 54, 56
reappearance of polio, 93
receptor site, 24, 86
recombinant vaccine, 41
recombination, 93
re-emerging infections,
    6, 93
REM sleep, 81
replication, 22–24
respiratory muscles, 76
rhinovirus, 86
risk factors, for PPS,
    75–76
Rockefeller Institute for
    Medical Research, 49
Roosevelt, Franklin Delano,
    20–22, 30, 57, 73, 74
Rudolph, Blanche, 60, 61
Rudolph, Wilma, 59–61
Ruma of Syria, 8, 9

Sabin, Albert, 17, 18, 39, 46,
    49–56
"Sabin Sunday", 54, 55
Sabin vaccine. *See* oral
    polio vaccine (OPV)
Salk, Jonas, 17, 39, 42–48
Salk polio vaccine. *See*
    inactivated poliovirus
    vaccine
sanitation, and polio
    immunity, 8–10, 50
Scott, Sir Walter, 11–13
sensitization, 35
Sesame Street, 62
sewage systems, 8–10
Shaw, Louis Agassiz, 27
sign, 104
Siptah (Egyptian pharaoh),
    8
sleep, 81

small intestine, 18
smallpox, 39, 99
smallpox vaccine, 35–39
Song Dynasty, 36
spasm, 19, 105
spinal cord, 26, 69
Stage IV (REM) sleep, 81
State University of New
    York at Stony Brook,
    82–84, 87
stele, 8
Strain I (Brunhilde), 50. *See
    also* paralytic polio
Strain II (Lansing), 50
Strain III (Leon), 50
stress, 69
subunit vaccine, 40, 105
Summer Olympics (Rome,
    1960), 60, 61
support, for weakened body
    parts, 81
Survival of the Wisest (Salk),
    48
swallowing, 75, 76
Swat Valley, Pakistan, 90–91
swimming, 73, 74
symptoms, 18–19, 27–30,
    105
syndrome, 105

Taliban, interference in
    polio vaccination by,
    90, 91
Tel Aviv Schulamit
    Academy, 62
temperature, for attenua-
    tion, 39, 40
tendonitis, 75
terrorism, 99. *See also* bio-
    terrorism
tetanus, 39, 105
Third World. *See* develop-
    ing world
tissue culture, 39
Townsville, Queensland,
    Australia polio clinic, 29
toxins, 39
toxoid, 40, 44, 105

About the Author

Dr. Alan Hecht is a practicing chiropractor in New York. He is also an adjunct professor at Farmingdale State College and Nassau Community College and an adjunct associate professor at the C.W. Post campus of Long Island University. He teaches courses in medical microbiology, anatomy and physiology, comparative anatomy, human physiology, embryology, and general biology. In addition, he is the course coordinator for human biology at Hofstra University where he is an adjunct assistant professor.

Dr. Hecht received his B.S. in biology–pre-medical studies from Fairleigh Dickinson University in Teaneck, New Jersey. He received his M.S. in basic medical sciences from New York University School of Medicine. He also received his Doctor of Chiropractic (D.C.) degree from New York Chiropractic College in Brookville, New York.

About the Consulting Editor

Hilary Babcock, M.D., M.P.H., is an assistant professor of medicine at Washington University School of Medicine and the medical director of occupational health for Barnes-Jewish Hospital and St. Louis Children's Hospital. She received her undergraduate degree from Brown University and her M.D. from the University of Texas Southwestern Medical Center at Dallas. After completing her residency, chief residency, and infectious disease fellowship at Barnes-Jewish Hospital, she joined the faculty of the infectious disease division. She completed a master's in public health from St. Louis University School of Public Health in 2006. She has lectured, taught, and written extensively about infectious diseases, their treatment, and their prevention. She is a member of numerous medical associations and is board certified in infectious diseases. She lives in St. Louis, Missouri.